Nonnative Speaker English Teachers

D1528757

"Researchers and educators will find this an essential reference book and an effective vehicle for introducing students to the Nonnative English Speaking Teacher research field."
Brock Brady, Education Sector Specialist, Peace Corps

"This book will definitely serve as a state-of-the-art resource for researchers in the field. I certainly welcome it."
Masaki Oda, Tamagawa University, Japan

"This is an exciting project. Many teacher training programs will find this book indispensable."
Peter Yongqi Gu, Victoria University of Wellington, New Zealand

According to current estimates, about 80% of English teachers worldwide are nonnative speakers of the language. The nonnative speaker movement began a decade ago to counter the discrimination faced by these teachers and to champion their causes. As the first single-authored volume on the topic since the birth of the movement, this book fills the need for a coherent account that

- traces the origins and growth of the movement
- summarizes the research that has been conducted
- highlights the challenges faced by nonnative speaker teachers
- promotes NNS teachers' professional growth

No discussion of World Englishes or the spread of English internationally is now complete without reference to the NNS movement. This book celebrates its first decade and charts a direction for its growth and development.

George Braine has taught English as a second/foreign language for more than 40 years.

ESL & Applied Linguistics Professional Series

Eli Hinkel, Series Editor

Visit **www.routledge.com/education** for additional information on titles in the ESL & Applied Linguistics Professional Series.

Nonnative Speaker English Teachers

Research, Pedagogy, and Professional Growth

George Braine
The Chinese University of Hong Kong

Routledge
Taylor & Francis Group
NEW YORK AND LONDON

First published 2010
by Routledge
270 Madison Avenue, New York, NY 10016

Simultaneously published in the UK
by Routledge
2 Park Square, Milton Park, Abingdon, Oxon OX14 4RN

Routledge is an imprint of the Taylor & Francis Group, an informa business

© 2010 Taylor & Francis

Typeset in Minion by Glyph International Ltd
Printed and bound in the United States of America on acid-free paper by Walsworth Publishing Company, Marceline, MO

Library of Congress Cataloging-in-Publication Data
Braine, George.
Nonnative speaker English teachers : research, pedagogy, and professional growth / George Braine.
p. cm. – (Esl & applied linguistics professional series)
Includes bibliographical references and index.
1. English teachers–Training of
2. English language–Study
and teaching–Foreign speakers.
3. Second language acquisition. I. Title.
PE1128.A2B66 2010
428.2'4–dc22

                                2009037534

ISBN10: (hbk) 0-415-87631-1
ISBN10: (pbk) 0-415-87632-X
ISBN10: (ebk) 0-203-85671-6

ISBN13: (hbk) 978-0-415-87631-5
ISBN13: (pbk) 978-0-415-87632-2
ISBN13: (ebk) 978-0-203-85671-0

For Miho

Contents

Preface

I am walking down a hallway during a TESOL convention. A young woman from an Asian country approaches, smiling shyly, and begins a conversation. She says how much my book *Non-native Educators in English Language Teaching* has meant to her. Soon, tears streaming down her face, she says that, as a non-native speaker studying in the United States to be an English teacher, she felt so much confused and alone. The struggle to keep up with her native speaker classmates seemed hopeless. She then read the book and realized that she wasn't alone, that others had struggled and triumphed before her, and that she had their support and guidance to succeed.

I am overwhelmed. The book was published in 1999. Just as it opened a floodgate of pent up emotions, *Non-native Educators in English Language Teaching* also gave rise to a multitude of other publications. The nonnative speaker movement that followed, while empowering these teachers, has also carved out a new area of scholarship in applied linguistics. The small group of TESOL members who planned and set up the Nonnative English Speakers in TESOL Caucus in 1998 could not have anticipated the energy, enthusiasm, and commitment that the Caucus would inspire, the research and publications it would generate, and the future leaders of TESOL it would foster.

Ten years on, it's time to look back and also to look forward. In order to maintain the momentum that was generated in the late 1990s, the nonnative speaker movement must now blaze new trails, publicizing its mission to all reaches of ELT, generating new areas for research, and inspiring new leaders across the ELT landscape. To some extent, that is the mission of this volume.

I first thought of *Nonnative Speaker English Teachers: Research, Pedagogy, and Professional Growth* more than five years ago but other commitments and distractions delayed its preparation. In hindsight, the delay was a blessing in disguise because much has occurred, in terms of leadership within TESOL Inc., a rapid growth in scholarship, and the evolution of the Caucus into an Interest Section. This volume is richer now than it would have been five years ago.

As always, I was not alone in this endeavor. My former research assistants, Sabina Mak, Liu Meihua, and Allen Ho performed the tedious task of gathering and summarizing publications relating to the contents of this volume.

My former student Wang Junju conducted the interview with the English teacher in China and had the transcript translated into English. He An E. and Jiang Changsheng helped by providing useful information on English teaching in China. During a particularly trying time, when my writing slowed down, Antonia Chandrasegaran generously hosted me to a weekend in Singapore where we gleefully explored the cuisine of Little India. Fawzia Braine proofread the draft. Finally, Matthew Sung helped me during the final stages of writing, downloading journal articles from the Internet, checking for references, and helping with the Index. As I worked on this volume, I felt they were watching over me, encouraging me on. I am grateful to them all.

Finally, I owe a special thanks to Naomi Silverman, my Editor. This is the third of my books she has edited. She welcomed all my book proposals, had them reviewed expeditiously, suggested marvelous subtitles, and was a steadying hand throughout. Perhaps unknowingly, she has provided a significant service to the nonnative speaker movement by publishing my books.

George Braine
Hong Kong

Introduction

According to current estimates, about 80% of the English teachers worldwide are nonnative speakers (NNS) of the language. Since 1999, through my publications and close association with the Nonnative Speaker Caucus within TESOL Inc., which in 2008 became an Interest Section, I have explored the issues relating to these teachers and promoted their causes. My 1999 anthology, *Non-native Educators in English Language Teaching*, is considered the forerunner of the NNS movement. Since its publication, three more anthologies on the topic have appeared: Kamhi-Stein (2004) *Learning and Teaching from Experience: Perspectives on Nonnative English-speaking Professionals*; Llurda (2005) *Non-native Language Teachers: Perceptions, Challenges, and Contributions to the Profession*; and Braine (2005) *Teaching English to the World*. In addition, nearly 200 journal articles, opinion pieces, and MA and Ph.D. dissertations have been written on the topic.

All four anthologies named above are edited volumes with chapters authored by various scholars. *Nonnative speaker English teachers: Research, pedagogy, and professional growth* will be the first single–authored volume on the topic since the NNS movement began. Now that the movement is a decade old, this volume will fulfill the need for a more coherent, book-length work, describing the growth of the movement, summarizing the research that has been conducted, highlighting the challenges faced by nonnative speaker teachers, and promoting their professional growth.

Over the past four decades, I have taught English from primary to university students both in Asia and North America, published extensively on topics relating to applied linguistics and English language teaching, edited two academic journals in the discipline, and been actively involved in international and local organizations linked to the profession. As a result, throughout this volume, a strong personal element based on my personal experiences will enrich the more academic contents in the text.

The opening chapter of *Nonnative Speaker English Teachers: Research, Pedagogy, and Professional Growth* is titled "The Nonnative Speaker Movement" and provides the background to the topic of the volume by tracing the history of English language teaching by NNS to the 15th Century. The roots of the current NNS movement are attributed to the concept of World Englishes first advocated in the 1970s. The movement's beginning and growth are then described and its achievements discussed under "A rise in self-esteem," "Surge in academic research and publications on NNS issues," and "Leadership in TESOL."

Chapter 2, "The Native Speaker–Nonnative Speaker Divide," is based on the premise that the classification of English teachers worldwide into native and nonnative speakers is a contentious issue that has drawn much attention in recent years. This chapter does not attempt to resolve the issue but provides a more rational basis for this classification and describes the challenges faced by NNS English teachers in the Inner, Outer, and Expanding Circles.

One outcome of the NNS movement is the impressive amount of research that has been conducted on the topic in the past decade. Most of this research has been on the self-perceptions of NNS teachers, and Chapter 3, "Research on Self-perceptions of NNS English Teachers," summarizes and analyzes the research conducted to date. While self-perceptions of teachers are important, the way in which students perceive them is also vital to these NNS teachers. Chapter 4, "Research on Students' Perceptions of NNS English Teachers," summarizes and analyzes the research on this aspect of NNS English teachers.

Although a considerable amount of research has been conducted on NNS issues, few biographies of individual teachers revealing their socioeconomic backgrounds, levels of education and training, and day-to-day association with the English language have been published. While enriching the research base on NNS English teachers, such narratives would also provide essential data for curriculum design and teacher education. Chapter 5, "An English Teacher from the Outer Circle," is the biography of an English teacher from Malaysia. To represent the Expanding Circle, a teacher from China was chosen because China is an ELT powerhouse, with an estimated 2 million English teachers and 300 million learners. Probably for the first time, Chapter 6, "An English Teacher from the Expanding Circle," provides insights into the life of an English teacher in China.

Chapter 7, "From Worlds Apart: The Lives of Two English Teachers," highlights the startling differences between the teachers from Malaysia and China. These differences are discussed and analyzed under headings such as "Socioeconomic backgrounds and early education," "Higher education," "Teaching and professional growth," and "Attitudes and perceptions." Chapter 7 also presents and analyzes further research on NNS English teachers that did not fall into the categories included in Chapters 5 and 6.

"Extrinsic and Intrinsic Challenges Faced by NNS English Teachers" is the title of Chapter 8. NNS teachers face numerous challenges in their profession, both due to their own shortcomings (such as low English proficiency) and those from external sources (such as students and parents who believe that native speaker teachers are automatically superior to their NNS counterparts). This chapter highlights and discusses such challenges.

As mentioned earlier, the NNS movement has grown rapidly in the past decade, mainly in the United States. Chapter 9, "Where Does the NNS Movement Go from Here?," charts a future course for the movement under headings such as "Enhancing the English language proficiency of NNS teachers," "Learning to collaborate with NS English teachers," "Making the most of professional organizations," and "Diversifying the scope of research on NNS English teachers." The final chapter, "Professional Development," offers advice on professional development, including how to find research topics, maintain working relationships with thesis supervisors, and specific advice on academic publishing.

Chapter 1

The Nonnative Speaker Movement

Teachers of English to Speakers of Other Languages, Inc. (TESOL) is the largest international organization of English teachers in the world. Currently, TESOL has over 11,000 members from 149 countries. TESOL is affiliated with 47 independent teachers' organizations in the United States and 50 similar organizations in other countries. As a result of these affiliations, the influence of TESOL extends to about 47,000 members worldwide (see www.tesol.org).

TESOL Quarterly, the research-oriented journal published by TESOL is probably the best-known academic journal in the field of applied linguistics. The journal, now in its 42nd volume, publishes four issues annually. Since its inception, the editor of *TESOL Quarterly* had been a native speaker of English. In 2005, the first nonnative speaker editor of *TESOL Quarterly* was appointed. Another dramatic change occurred in the leadership of TESOL the following year. Since its incorporation in 1966, the president of TESOL, too, had been a native speaker of English. But, in 2006, the first nonnative president was elected by the organization's general membership.

These two unprecedented events are an indicator of the recognition that nonnative speaker (NNS) English teachers have received from the mainstream and the empowerment that the NNS teachers have themselves achieved in recent years. No discussion of such recognition and empowerment can proceed without reference to the NNS movement that arose within the past decade. This movement, which saw its origins in the United States, has since drawn the attention of English teachers and scholars worldwide. As a result, no discussion of World Englishes or the spread of English internationally is now complete without reference to the NNS movement.

Background

Historical evidence suggests that English was being taught as a second or foreign language as far back as the 15th century. During the 16th century, the rise of England as a maritime power and the expansion of the British Empire led to the recognition of English as an important language alongside French, Italian, and Latin, and to a growing interest in learning English. Gabriel Meurier, a

Frenchman who lived in Antwerp, may have been the first NNS teacher of English we know by name. *A Treatise for to Learn to Speak French and English*, authored by Meurier, was published in 1553 (Howatt, 1984). In the latter half of the 16th century, when a large number of refugees from Flanders, France, Italy, and Spain settled in England, some who taught English to these settlers were themselves refugees or immigrants and therefore NNS of English. The best-known among them, Jaques Bellot, taught English to the French community in the London area and authored two books, *The English Schoolmaster* (1580), and *Familiar Dialogues* (1586). Two other well-known immigrant language teachers of this period were Claudius Holyband, a Frenchman, and John Florio, an Italian (see Howatt, 1984 for detailed accounts of their work). With this tangible evidence of English being taught in England by NNS of the language, we may safely assume that the rapid spread of English from the 16th century would have spawned a parallel growth in English language teaching, and enterprising NNS may have been quick to assume the role of teachers in other countries too.

The British Council (www.britishcouncil.org/english/engfaqs.htm) estimates that English is spoken as the second language by about 375 million speakers and as a foreign language by about 750 million speakers. There is little doubt that the majority of English teachers are NNS because these vast numbers of second and foreign language speakers would be taught mainly by indigenous NNS English teachers. For instance, China recently made English a compulsory subject from Grade 3 onwards. According to recent statistics, about 230 million students were enrolled in primary, secondary, and tertiary level in China (see http://www.edu.cn/jiao_yu_fa_zhan_498/20080901/t20080901_321919. shtml). Undoubtedly, the majority of these students are taught by Chinese teachers of English.

Despite the strong presence of NNS English teachers worldwide, issues relating to them were not openly discussed or studied till a little more than a decade ago. This may have been because the topic is unusually sensitive and may have been considered politically incorrect. The commonly accepted view in language pedagogy has been that NNS teachers are second in knowledge and performance to native speaker (NS) teachers (Phillipson, 1992 has discussed the origins of this issue). While the authority of the NS was accepted as the norm in English-speaking countries, there appeared to be power struggles between the expatriate NS teachers and the indigenous NNS teachers in EFL contexts (see Canagarajah, 1999, for instance).

The roots of the NNS movement probably lie with the concept of World Englishes first proposed by Braj Kachru and Larry Smith in the 1970s and since accepted widely by linguists. Kachru's classification of the spread of English into three concentric circles was groundbreaking because, for the first time, it showed that the NNS in the Outer and Expanding Circles far outnumbered the NS of English in the Inner Circle. Kachru (1992) later argued that the dichotomy between native and NNS of English is functionally uninsightful and linguistically questionable, especially in the context of the functions of the English language in multilingual societies.

If NNS English teachers needed consciousness raising, it came with the publication of Robert Phillipson's *Linguistic Imperialism* in 1992. One topic that Phillipson dealt with was what he termed the "native speaker fallacy"—the belief that "the ideal teacher of English is a native speaker"—which he speculated may have had its origins at the *Commonwealth Conference on the Teaching of English as a Second Language*, held in 1962. The result of this tenet was the widely held assumption that NS English teachers are better than NNS teachers. This "superiority" of NS teachers had been bolstered by Chomsky's (1965) notions that the native speaker is the authority on language and that he/she is the ideal informant on grammar. Phillipson (1992) challenged the fallacy by stating that NS abilities could be instilled in NNS through teacher training, that NNS of a language have undergone the process of learning a (second) language and are therefore better qualified to teach the language, and that language teaching is no longer synonymous with the teaching of culture, and thus could be taught by teachers who did not share the same culture as the language they taught.

One of the first to explore NNS teacher issues was Peter Medgyes, himself a NNS from Hungary, who advanced three hypotheses based on his assumption that NS and NNS teachers are "two different species" (1994): native and NNS teachers differ in terms of language proficiency and teaching practice (behavior); most of the differences in teaching practice could be attributed to the discrepancy in language proficiency; and both NS and NNS could be equally good teachers on their own terms. However, Medgyes' publications were based in Britain and were largely unknown in the United States, where the NNS movement had its origins.

Birth of the Nonnative Speaker Movement

The beginning of the nonnative speaker movement was the colloquium titled "In Their Own Voices: Nonnative Speaker Professionals in TESOL", which I organized at the 30th Annual TESOL Convention held in Chicago in 1996. I invited well-known NNS scholars in applied linguistics as well as novices to our profession—Ulla Connor, Suresh Canagarajah, Kamal Sridhar, Jacinta Thomas, and Devi Chitrapu—to address issues that were of concern to them. They exceeded my expectations, presenting highly charged, mainly personal, narratives. The colloquium generated much enthusiasm among the audience and the idea for a TESOL Caucus for NNS was first proposed at the discussion that followed. The statement that was written in order to launch the signature drive to establish the colloquium can be found on page 111 in Bailey, Curtis, & Nunan (2001).

Around this time, I was invited to write an article for the TESOL organization's newspaper *TESOL Matters*, and it was published as "NNS and Invisible Barriers in ELT" (Braine, 1998). In the article, I stated that for many NNS

English teachers, qualifications, ability, and experience were of little help in the job market where the invisible rule appeared to be "No NNS need apply." I pointed out that despite the TESOL organization's explicit opposition to hiring practices that discriminate against NNS, most ELT administrators did not hire NNS. I described two frequent excuses trotted out for not hiring NNS—that ESL students prefer being taught by NS and that recruiting foreigners involves a complex legal process—but argued that the main reason was the subtle opposition to the increasing presence of foreigners in western academia as teachers, researchers, and scholars. Although a similar presence of foreigners/NNS in English language teaching was only to be expected—there are at least four NNS to every native speaker of English—it met with opposition when scarce jobs were threatened.

I also pointed out that this was especially ironic in ELT, considering the profession's strident championing of multiculturalism, diversity, and other sociopolitical causes on behalf of ESL students and immigrants. While ESL students were praised and admired for the multiculturalism and diversity they bring into language classes, NNS English teachers who could also contribute their rich multicultural, multilingual experiences were often barred from the same classes.

In another ironic phenomenon, NNS English teachers who return to their countries after obtaining higher degrees and teacher qualifications in the West are not always able to find work. Some language program administrators—notably in Japan, Korea, and Hong Kong, for instance—appeared to prefer unqualified NS of English instead of qualified local teachers. I stated that such teachers were in the bewildering and frustrating position of being denied what they had been trained to do.

In 1998, the Non-Native English Speakers in TESOL (NNEST) Caucus was established with myself as the chair, Jun Liu as the chair-elect, Lia Kamhi-Stein as the newsletter editor, and Aya Matsuda as the web master. The first formal meeting of the Caucus was held at the TESOL Convention in 1999, which coincided with the publication of my book *Non-Native Educators in English Language Teaching*. The overall aim of the Caucus was to strengthen effective teaching and learning of English around the world while respecting individuals' language rights. Specifically, the major goals were to

- create a nondiscriminatory professional environment for all TESOL members regardless of native language and place of birth
- encourage the formal and informal gatherings of NNS at TESOL and affiliate conferences
- encourage research and publications on the role of nonnative speaker teachers in ESL and EFL contexts, and
- promote the role of nonnative speaker members in TESOL and affiliate leadership positions.

The Caucus used a biannual newsletter, an active listserv, and the website to publicize its activities and disseminate information among the membership. The website also listed a bibliography of publications that have appeared under the topic. The Caucus was fortunate in the leaders it elected and the enthusiasm and dedication of its members. For those of us who have been members from its inception, the Caucus appeared to have released a floodgate of pent-up energy in the empowerment of NNS. Through outreach activities, well-attended meetings, an actively subscribed listserv, conference presentations, and publications, the Caucus created a vibrant TESOL community that had attracted 1,700 members by 2008.

In 2008, by consensus of its members, the Caucus transformed itself into an Interest Section of the TESOL organizations. Caucuses are mainly for advocacy whereas Interest Sections are more concerned with professional issues. This transition marked another milestone of the movement with its emergence as a full-fledged area of research.

Reflecting on Achievements

Ten years after the formation of the Caucus, it is time to reflect on the achievements of the NNS movement. What began as an attempt by a small group of TESOL members has now become a worldwide movement. Three of the original objectives—to encourage the formal and informal gatherings of NNS at TESOL and affiliate conferences; to encourage research and publications on the role of nonnative speaker teachers in ESL and EFL contexts; and to promote the role of nonnative speaker members in TESOL and affiliate leadership positions—have been achieved beyond expectations. The first objective—to create a nondiscriminatory professional environment for all TESOL members regardless of native language and place of birth—is more an ideal than a pragmatic reality, and the NNS movement will continue to work towards these ends. More specifically, the major achievements are the rise in self-esteem, a surge in academic research and publications on NNS issues, and leadership in TESOL. I will now consider these achievements in more detail.

Rise in Self-Esteem

When I was contemplating a suitable name for the Caucus in 1997–98, I thought of "NNS in TESOL", and sought the opinion of others interested in forming the Caucus. Some colleagues did not support the inclusion of the term "nonnative speaker" in the name and suggested alternatives (see Chapter 2 for a list of suggested names). I was not surprised at their reticence in using the term "nonnative speaker." As stated earlier, NNS English teachers had long being considered second rate, which in turn may have caused a certain lack of self-confidence among NNS teachers. To my recollection, till the formation of the Caucus, few NNS English teachers had called themselves NNS, either in academic presentations or publications. The term "nonnative speaker" was indeed a pejorative. In fact, one NNS scholar also stated that "to call ourselves non-NS [in naming the Caucus] is akin to the slave owner's language."

In sharp contrast, the past ten years have seen a surge in the use of the term "nonnative speaker" in scholarly presentations and publications as well as in informal discussions, both face-to-face and online. Now, it is politically correct to use the term, and NS scholars and teachers no longer hesitate to use it. But, among NNS, the change has been dramatic. No longer afraid to call themselves NNS, they have transformed the landscape of academic presentations and publications. For instance, since the formation of the Caucus, the annual TESOL conventions have included about 15–20 presentations on NNS issues with the term "NNS" in the title. Many of these presentations have been from NNS themselves. The 2008 New York TESOL convention, for instance, saw more than 25 presentations affiliated to the Caucus, many by NNS with "NNS" in the title.

This does not mean that the term has gained unanimous acceptance within the NNS community. During the transition from a Caucus to an Interest Section, the debate on the term was re-ignited, with a number of members arguing that it was an opportunity to substitute a more suitable term. I took the opposing view, mainly because a large body of research relating to NNS would be lost or sidelined if there was a name change.

Surge in Academic Research and Publications on NNS Issues

The NNS bibliography, available on the Interest Section website, lists more than 200 publications. Most of them have appeared since the formation of the Caucus and many have been authored by NNS. Since the appearance of *Non-native Educators in English Language Teaching* (Braine, 1999), three major anthologies have also been published. They are *Learning and Teaching from Experience: Perspectives on Nonnative English-speaking Professionals* (2004), edited by Lia Kamhi-Stein; *Non-native Language Teachers: Perceptions, Challenges, and Contributions to the Profession* (2005), edited by Enric Llurda; and *Teaching English to the World: History, Curriculum, and Practice* (2005), edited by George Braine. The contributors to Braine (1999) and Kamhi-Stein (2004) were mainly from the USA, and to Llurda (2005) mainly from Europe. The 2005 anthology by Braine consisted of chapters authored by NNS authors from Asia, Europe, and Latin America.

Language Teaching, now in Volume 41, publishes state-of-the-art articles on topics/areas related to second language teaching and learning. The publication of a state-of-the-art article on a particular topic or area is an acknowledgment that it has received wide acceptance in second language teaching and learning circles and that it has a sufficient body of research to warrant publication.

In Volume 41(3) of *Language Teaching*, the state-of-the-art article was "Nonnative English-speaking English language teachers: History and research", authored by Lucie Moussu and Enric Llurda. This publication could be seen as a milestone in, and the coming of age of, the nonnative speaker movement. This article has 165 items in the list of references, a rich source of information for future researchers and scholars. The same volume of *Language Teaching* also carries a comprehensive review by Amir H. Soheili-Mehr of the anthologies by Braine (2005), Kamhi-Stein (2004) and Llurda (2005), as well as of Davies (2003).

Leadership in TESOL

As mentioned earlier, Suresh Canagarajah, a NNS, now edits *TESOL Quarterly*, and another, Jun Liu,[1] was elected President of TESOL for 2006–07. Canagarajah was a presenter at the historic TESOL colloquium of 1996, and Liu is a founding member of the NNEST Caucus and was its second Chair. The third Chair of the Caucus, Lia Kamhi-Stein, has served as a Board member of TESOL. Another active member of the Caucus, Brock Brady, has also been a TESOL board member and, at the time of writing, is the President Elect of TESOL. In addition, more and more NNS are taking leadership roles in applied linguistics and English language teaching.

Chapter 2

The Native Speaker—Nonnative Speaker Divide

As I stated in the Introduction, I have no wish to explore the NS and NNS debate, which, in my view, is unlikely ever to be resolved. In simplistic terms, a NS of a language is one who speaks the language as his/her first language; accordingly, a NNS is one who speaks that language as a second or foreign language. In learning a language, one attempts to replicate the shared system of the speakers of that language. When learning English as the first language, the assumption is that learners attempt to replicate the shared system of fellow NS. In the case of second or foreign language learners, the replication is the shared system of fellow NNS, which is often an approximation of the shared system of NS.

However, the NS/NNS distinction is not as simple as that. The term "native speaker" undoubtedly has positive connotations: it denotes a birthright, fluency, cultural affinity, and sociolinguistic competence. In contrast, the term "nonnative speaker" carries the burden of the minority, of marginalization and stigmatization, with resulting discrimination in the job market and in professional advancement.

In *The Native Speaker in Applied Linguistics* (1991), Davies claims that no proper definition of a "native speaker" exists. A similar claim could be made for the term "nonnative speaker" too. In the previous chapter, I mentioned that some NNS wished to avoid the "nonnative speaker" label in the names proposed for the TESOL Caucus. Because the struggle for identity by NNS continues, the alternative terms that were proposed are worth listing again here: second language speaking professional, English teachers speaking other languages, and second language teaching professionals.

In some instances, the distinction between NS and NNS blurs. When Inbar-Lourie (2001) investigated why some teachers in Israel perceived themselves as NS of English, she found that the teachers' self-perceptions could be explained by nine variables, two of which could best predict this self-identity: having spoken English from the age of 0 to 6, and others' perceptions of them as NS of English. To some degree these findings support the most obvious (and superficial) ways in which NS and NNS are identified: by country of origin, names, ethnicity, skin color, and accent. The Chinese-American writer Maxine Hong Kingston (1977) refers to being complimented on speaking English well. In his autobiographical novel *Turning Japanese* (1991), David Mura, a third-generation American who taught Freshman English, mentions being mistaken for a NNS by his teaching assistant.

Nonnative Speaker English Teachers in the Inner Circle

The confusion regarding their identity and, by extension, their status is more of an issue for NNS teachers in countries where English is the dominant language. When English was first taught in these "Inner Circle" (Kachru, 1992) countries—such as Australia, Britain, the USA—to students from other countries and to recent immigrants, the teachers were mainly indigenous, Caucasian, NS of the language. But, due to two reasons, the situation began to change gradually. First, recent immigrants who had been teachers of English in their home countries began to apply for English teaching positions in Inner Circle countries at primary and secondary schools as well as at vocational schools and community colleges. Second, as more and more universities in these countries started teacher-training programs in English as a second language (mainly at the Master's level, usually referred to as MATESOL), some graduates of these programs began to apply for positions available locally. These applicants were even more eligible for these jobs because they had a recognized qualification, and in most cases, some local teaching experience through a practicum.

However, especially in the early years, these NNS applicants met with stiff resistance from employers. There appeared to be an unwritten rule: "No NNS need apply for English teaching positions." Administrators of intensive English programs (that cater mainly to international students with a low proficiency in English) were the most resistant and sometimes stated their opposition openly at professional conferences and job interviews. According to these administrators, students in intensive English programs had come to the US to be taught by NS teachers; if they wished to be taught by NNS, as they were in their home countries, there was no need to come to the US. This argument has some merit, as my own experience described while teaching at an intensive English program shows: two international students, both NNS, complained to the director of the program about my accent and wished to be moved to a class taught by NS teachers (see Braine, 1999).

A study by Mahboob, Uhrig, Newman, & Hartford (2004) indicates that NNS teachers are still a minority in these intensive English programs. Of the 1,425 teachers employed in the 118 intensive English programs they surveyed, only 112 were NNS and most of them had been hired as part-timers. According to the majority of program administrators, NS status was an important criterion in the hiring of English teachers in these intensive programs.

A survey conducted by Clark & Paran (2007) among English language teaching institutions in the UK showed that the "native English speaker" criterion was judged either moderately or very important by 72% of the 90 responding administrators. This applied to the whole sample of respondents as well as to the separate groups of private language schools only and universities only. Clarke & Paran conclude that the "native English speaker criterion" thus excludes competent English language teachers from being considered for employment.

In recent years, NNS English teachers, especially those who teach or have taught in the USA, have gained the confidence to publicize their grievances. My own writing on the topic (Braine, 1998), described in Chapter 1, was probably the first public airing of this complaint. Since then, NNS English teachers have been openly discussing discrimination they have faced from employers, fellow teachers, students, and parents of students. These discussions continue to occur informally at conference venues, listservs, and on Internet sites. *Essential Teacher* magazine, published quarterly by TESOL Inc., is distributed to all TESOL members and therefore has a large, international readership. Recently, two NNS English teachers—Faiza Derbel and Yujong Park—have described their negative experiences in *Essential Teacher*, thereby reaching a wide readership. Derbel (2005), an Arab and a Muslim, was told that she could not be hired to teach first-year writing courses because she was not a NS. She says that, in addition to the discrimination she suffered, the silence of her TESOL colleagues and advisors was bewildering and disheartening. Park (2006), who came to the US with seven years' experience in her native Korea, was told that ESL instructor positions were open only to NS of English.

TESOL Inc., the largest organization of English teachers in North America, took an early stand on nonnative teachers and hiring practices. In a statement issued in October 1991, TESOL resolved to expunge discriminatory language from its publications and to prevent discrimination in employment practices. To its credit, TESOL has enforced these resolutions strictly, and, at least in the US, a discriminatory job advertisement is rarely seen. TESOL Inc. has reiterated its position with another statement in 2006.

Nonnative Speaker English Teachers in the Outer and Expanding Circles

But in countries where English is spoken as a second or foreign language—"Outer Circle" and "Expanding Circle" countries in Kachru's (1992) terms—and where local NNS English teachers have to compete for jobs with NS, the prejudices, discrimination, and rivalries continue to exist. But, expatriate NS teachers are not present in all these countries. Instead, their presence is determined by one important criterion: the relative affluence of the country in question. Take the case of Asia. In countries that have a relatively low per capita income—such as Bangladesh, Cambodia, India, Indonesia, Pakistan,

Sri Lanka, and Vietnam—there is hardly any rivalry because no expatriate teachers would be attracted to public school salaries that pay as little as the equivalent of US$50 per month. However, the increasing prosperity of the middle class even in these countries, that has led to the growth of so-called "international schools", has opened the way for NS "traveling teachers" to find lucrative employment. But, in more prosperous locations such as Hong Kong, Japan, and Korea, where salaries are much higher, hiring practices can be openly discriminatory. Table 2.1 below shows the annual per capita income of some Asian countries.

One of the primary sources of information for NS of English looking for teaching positions abroad is TransitionsAbroad.com, described as a portal for paid and volunteer work, residence, study, as well as cultural travel overseas. In an entry titled "Teaching English in Asia: Where and How to Find ESL Jobs", by Susan Griffith, a contributing editor for *Transitions Abroad*, the subtitles are revealing: "China: An explosion of private language schools"; "Indonesia: Foreign teachers receive ten times local wage"; "Taiwan: Only requirements are a college degree and a pulse"; "Thailand: Teaching jobs are virtually guaranteed"; and "South Asia: Teaching jobs scarce because of poverty." To quote Griffith further:

> In Korea, Taiwan, Japan, Thailand and, increasingly, China, a high proportion of the population are eager for tuition from English speakers. A university degree in any subject is the only prerequisite, though in some cases just a degree of enthusiasm will suffice.

In the context of the NS–NNS divide within the Outer Circle, I will describe this situation with reference to Hong Kong, where I have lived and worked for the past 14 years. Hong Kong became a colony of Britain in 1842 and was

Table 2.1 What attracts traveling NS English teachers?

Country/region	Annual per capita income in US$ (2007)
Bangladesh	$470
Cambodia	$430
China	$1,740
Hong Kong	$27,690
India	$730
Indonesia	$1,260
Japan	$38,950
Korea	$15,880
Singapore	$24,220
Sri Lanka	$1,170
Taiwan	$16,590

Source: http://www.finfacts.com/biz10/globalworldincomepercapita.htm

returned to China only in 1997. As a legacy of this colonial rule, English remains an official language alongside Chinese. Because of its role as an international financial center, Hong Kong attracts a large number of expatriate professionals from North America, Europe, and Asia. As far as NS of English are concerned, in addition to British citizens, there is a significant presence of Americans, Australians, Canadians, New Zealanders, and South Africans in Hong Kong. The prominent role given to the English language under colonial rule—in government, business, and professional sectors, as well as in higher education—remains to this day. Although laws against discriminatory hiring practices exist in Hong Kong, they do not relate to linguistic background or ethnic origin. To their credit, universities and other institutions funded by the government do not mention these factors when they hire teaching staff.

However, since 1987, even the Hong Kong government has employed NS teachers in secondary schools, giving the so-called Native-speaking English Teacher (NET) scheme wide publicity (see http://www.edb.gov.hk/). The scheme, first introduced in 1987, was later extended to primary schools as well. Under the scheme, at least one NS teacher is provided for every government secondary school, while primary schools may have to share teachers. The attractive salaries (up to US$5,800 per month for secondary teachers and US$4,800 for primary teachers) and travel, baggage, and rental allowances have attracted teachers from Australia, Canada, New Zealand, the UK, and the USA to the scheme.

Although the government claims that the scheme is a success, a study by Boyle (1997) and more focused research (Cheung, 2002; Lee, 2004) indicate that the scheme has a number of shortcomings. From the viewpoint of a local teacher, the scheme has been criticized for marginalizing, demoralizing, and diminishing the usefulness of local NNS English teachers (Lung, 1999). This is partly because the NS teachers are required to act as advisors or "resource persons" for local teachers. Above all, the very fact that NS teachers need to be hired after more than 150 years of close association with the English language reveals the failure of English language education in Hong Kong.

If the hiring of NS teachers by the government was bad enough, the openly discriminatory situation in the local private sector for English teachers is truly despairing, especially to someone who has championed the cause of NNS teachers. The leading English language newspaper in Hong Kong, the *South China Morning Post*, prints job advertisements in its Saturday edition. Numerous positions are advertised for teachers of English from kindergarten to secondary level, mainly at privately owned schools and tutorial centers. The discrimination, prejudice, and the political incorrectness of these advertisements would be astonishing to a reader used to equal opportunity in employment. The headings make no bones about the primary qualification for the position: "native English teacher," "native teachers," "native-speaking English teachers," "native English private tutor." On a recent Saturday, only one advertisement mentioned the term "qualified" in the heading. Most often, the qualities required are the ability to "teach with fun," being "cheerful and enthusiastic," or "patient and loving." Academic qualifications are not always mentioned, but a "British accent" is a must for some jobs. The English department of the Chinese University of Hong Kong, where I teach, graduates a number of MA and Master of Philosophy students every year. Many of them seek teaching positions. To my knowledge, none has been able to find a position at a private school because of the preference for NS teachers.

In a letter to the Editor of the *South China Morning Post*, Suresh (2000) poignantly expressed the frustration experienced by NNS applicants for English teaching positions. When Suresh arrived in Hong Kong, he had been speaking English for 43 years in India, Singapore, Australia, and the US. He had an Australian passport and a Master's (degree) in English with more than seven years' teaching experience in California. Yet whenever he answered a job advertisement in Hong Kong for an English teaching position, and the prospective employer saw his name on the application or saw his skin color, the response was, "Oh, we're really looking for a native English speaker." Suresh, who claims to have been "living and loving" the English language—"speaking, reading, writing, and thinking in English"—was baffled by his rejection and pointed out that the "native speaker" label stands for Caucasians only.

As mentioned earlier, this preference for NS English teachers becomes more apparent with growing affluence. China is now emerging as a powerhouse in English language teaching. English has been made a compulsory language from primary school and is required of all students at tertiary level. Next to India, China has the largest number of English learners and teachers in the world. At one time, due to its low per capita income, scarce resources, and rudimentary living conditions, the only NS English teachers that China could attract were volunteers from English-speaking countries. However, with increasing affluence, Chinese institutions are now able to hire native speaker teachers with attractive salaries, travel allowances, and other fringe benefits.

As Oda (1999) has pointed out repeatedly, the NS–NNS divide occasionally spills over to professional associations as well. Describing the situation within the Japan Association for Language Teaching (JALT) in the mid-1990s,[1] Oda points out that, although 45% of the members of JALT were Japanese nationals who were NNS of English, JALT adopted a policy of English monolingualism in terms of officers' duties, elections, conferences, research grants, and decision-making that disadvantaged NNS of English.

Earlier, I mentioned that the sensitive and politically incorrect nature of the NS–NNS divide kept the topic from being discussed till Phillipson (1992) and Medgyes (1994). An even more disconcerting offshoot of this divide, especially when it comes to employment, is the inherent racism, white vs. black, brown, or yellow. In a glaring headline titled "Asian English teachers demand action on racial discrimination," Hong Kong's *South China Morning Post* (Heron, 2006) presented statistics provided by a local recruitment agency for English language teachers. The records of the agency for the previous two years, covering 525 private English language centers and 397 individual clients seeking private tutoring, showed that 67% of the language centers and 43% of clients seeking private tutoring only requested the services of Caucasian teachers. In terms of obtaining employment, the statistics showed that more than twice as many Caucasian teachers were successful when compared to Asian teachers. In terms of salary, Caucasian female teachers were paid HK$47 (US$6) more per hour than their Asian counterparts. According to the director of the employment agency, "Ethnic Chinese people are refused employment opportunities immediately upon revelation of their last name or photo." Private language centers, according to the director, "often indicate they will not consider interviewing those of Asian descent" (p. E3). In a subsequent issue of the newspaper, Andy Kirkpatrick, a senior academic at a local institution, took the initiative to comment on this issue. In a letter to the Editor titled "Blatant racism in the teaching of English," Kirkpatrick (2006) stated that, for a long period, "nonwhite teachers who are both professionally trained and have excellent English proficiency have been subject to racial discrimination" (p. E4). In support of his position that the English language teaching profession should discard the "native speaker" mentality, Kirkpatrick outlined seven criteria for evaluating the competence of English language teachers.

As far as the Expanding Circle is concerned, China offers the most vivid instances of discrimination in the employment of NNS English teachers. I stated earlier that NS English teachers were attracted to countries with high per capita incomes such as Hong Kong, Japan, and South Korea. Table 2.1 also showed that the per capita income of China was only US$1,290. However, these official figures hide an enormous gulf that exists between the extremely affluent Chinese citizens—for the most part residents of cities like Beijing, Shanghai, and Guangzhou—and the rural poor, many scratching a subsistence living as peasant farmers or laborers.

With China's entry into the World Trade Organization (WTO) and its hosting of the Olympic Games, it is reportedly suffering from *yingwen re* or "English fever" of epidemic proportions (see Shao, 2005). Fewer people are seeking comparatively low-paying government jobs; instead, more educated Chinese are seeking lucrative positions in joint-venture companies that require fluency in English. Although the exact number of English learners in China is not known, an approximate number may be arrived at by calculating the number of schools, institutions, and students at primary, secondary, and tertiary level. According to the latest statistics, China has more than 230,000 primary schools, 90,000 junior middle and senior middle schools, and 2,300 tertiary institutions. About 230 million students were enrolled in these schools and institutions (see http://www.edu.cn/jiao_yu_fa_zhan_498/20080901/t20080901_321919.shtml). Considering that English is taught from Grade 3 onwards, a conservative estimate of the number of English learners in China's schools and universities would be around 300 million, although Niu & Wolff (2004) have doubled this figure to 600 million learners.

The affluent Chinese, especially those who attend private language schools to learn English—and, according to *Transitions Abroad,* these schools have seen "an explosion" in terms of their numbers—appear to suffer not only from "English fever" but also from the "native speaker fallacy." While Caucasian teachers from the USA, Canada, Britain, Australia, and New Zealand are welcomed at these schools, American-born Chinese who are NS of English or who have native-level proficiency face discrimination in terms of employment. Shao (2005), a Chinese American qualified in TESOL and fluent in Mandarin Chinese, recalls her experiences while attempting to find an English teaching position in China. Despite her optimism and enthusiasm at the beginning of her job search, she is soon discouraged by a former classmate, herself a Chinese who has returned to China, who advises Shao not to come to China to teach English because discrimination against non-Caucasian teachers is strong and "most colleges, universities, and language institutions prefer white only." Shao is warned that, although she is an American citizen, she would be paid less than other NS of English because she is ethnically Chinese. Shao also received similarly discouraging advice from a teacher recruiter based in the US and a student from China; visits to a few websites offering advice to English teachers planning to work in China only reinforced the negativity. Shao, however, ends on a positive note, vowing to be the most qualified NNS English teacher to "show students, school administrators, parents, and fellow teachers [in China] … that nonnative speaker teachers are indeed qualified and competent teachers."

Shao's (2005) views are reinforced by Hsu (2005), another Chinese American who actually visited China searching for an English teaching position. Writing in Hong Kong's *South China Morning Post,* Hsu described the difficulties he faced, having to go through "rejection after rejection, with replies such as 'You know, now in China, many students want their foreign teachers to have a white face'" (Hsu, 2005). Not mincing his words, Hsu accuses the English language teaching situation in China of being racist, where the "Chinese discriminate against their own kind" in favor of Caucasian teachers.

Chapter 3

Research on Self-perceptions of NNS English Teachers

In Chapter 1 I noted the surge of research studies connected to NNS English teachers, mostly conducted since the beginning of the NNS movement. Although some of these studies remain unpublished theses at the Master's and doctoral level, many have been published as chapters in anthologies or as journal articles. In this chapter, as well as in Chapters 4 and 7, I will summarize these studies and attempt to determine their implications for NNS English teachers in particular, and to the English-language teaching profession in general. In this chapter, I will summarize the research on the self-perceptions of NNS English teachers.

No review of research into NNS English teachers could begin without reference to Peter Medgyes, who appears to be the first to have brought the issues concerning NNS English teachers into the open. His two articles in the *ELT Journal* titled "The schizophrenic teacher" (1983) and "Native or nonnative: Who's worth more?" (1992) were the forerunners of his groundbreaking book *The Non-native Teacher*, first published by Macmillan in 1994 and reissued by Hueber in 1999, in which Medgyes mixed research with his own experience as a NNS English teacher and teacher educator, and his observations of other NNS teachers and boldly discussed previously untouched topics that would be considered controversial even today: "Natives and nonnatives in opposite trenches," "The dark side of being a nonnative," and "Who's worth more: the native or the nonnative." Medgyes also advanced four hypotheses based on his assumption that NS and NNS English teachers are "two different species" (p. 25): that the NS and NNS teachers differ in terms of (1) language proficiency; (2) teaching practice (behavior); that (3) most of the differences in teaching practice can be attributed to the discrepancy in language proficiency; and that (4) both types of teachers can be equally good teachers on their own terms.

Perhaps the first empirical study of self-perceptions of NNS English teachers was that of Reves & Medgyes (1994), for which they surveyed 216 English teachers from 10 countries (Brazil, Czechoslovakia, Hungary, Israel, Mexico, Nigeria, Russia, Sweden, Yugoslavia, and Zimbabwe). An overwhelming majority of the subjects, nearly 92%, by their own admission were NNS of English. The teachers spoke 19 different first/native languages. The objective was to examine the following hypothesis: NS and NNS English teachers differ in terms of their teaching practice (behaviors); these differences in teaching practice are mainly due to their differing levels of language proficiency; and their knowledge of these differences affects the NNS teachers' "self-perception and teaching attitudes" (p. 354). The questionnaire consisted of 23 items of which 18 were addressed to both NS and NNS, and five to NNS only. Most of the questions were close-ended and meant to elicit personal information of the teachers and their teaching contexts.

The open-ended questions were meant to elicit the teachers' self-perceptions and their opinions relating to the three hypotheses. According to the teachers, in terms of teaching behavior, the NS teachers used "more real, unhampered natural language" (p. 360) during their teaching. On the other hand, the NNS teachers were "preoccupied with accuracy, more formal features of English" (p. 360), while lacking in fluency and more sophisticated semantic usage. Because these teachers are unsure of appropriate language use, they tend to overuse formal registers. On the positive side, NNS teachers had "deeper insights into the English language" (p. 361), appeared to be better qualified than their NS counterparts, and showed more empathy towards their students with whom they shared a common first language. Because of their shared linguistic, cultural, and educational backgrounds, these NNS teachers had a better ability to read the minds of their students and predict their difficulties.

Thirty-five percent of the teachers surveyed rarely or never interacted with NS of English, and 37% admitted that their command of English was average, poor, or very poor. Eighty-four percent of the NNS teachers admitted to having difficulties with the English language, vocabulary and fluency being the most common areas followed by speaking, pronunciation, and listening comprehension. Nearly 70% of the subjects stated that their language difficulties had hampered their teaching effectiveness. Analyzing the responses of the teachers, Reves & Medgyes speculate that teaching qualifications, time spent in an English-speaking country, the frequency of the teachers' contact with NS of English, their knowledge of professional organizations, and "some conditions under which they teach" (p. 357) would affect their command of English and thus their self-image. The higher the NNS teachers' proficiency in English, "the less self-conscious, hesitant, and insecure" (p. 364) they would be. In order to "salvage" these teachers' self-perceptions, two steps are recommended: an open acknowledgement of the differences in language proficiency of NS and NNS English teachers, and renewed efforts to improve their English proficiency. Further, in order to enhance the self-perception, NNS teachers should be made aware of their advantages as language teachers.

In a study conducted in Hong Kong, Andrews (1994) investigated the awareness and knowledge of English grammar by surveying 141 local ESL teachers and teacher trainees. Part of the survey consisted of questions to determine the teachers' confidence in teaching grammar. The subjects included

101 NNS teachers (all native Cantonese speakers) and 29 NS English teachers. The NNS teachers were of the view that it was more useful to memorize grammar rules than to practice communication. NNS teachers with a tertiary level education had more confidence in their knowledge of grammar. Further, those with more than six years' teaching experience expressed more confidence in understanding and applying grammar rules.

Nuzhat Amin, herself a NNS, originally from Pakistan, interviewed five minority female teachers in Canada who had adult ESL students from various racial, cultural, and linguistics backgrounds (1997). All the teachers had immigrated to Canada as adults. The aim of the interviews was to determine these teachers' perceptions of their students' ideal ESL teacher. According to the teachers, some ESL students make two general assumptions: that only Caucasians can be native speakers of English, and that only native speakers know "real," "proper," "Canadian" English. As a result, the teachers were often compared unfavorably with Caucasian teachers, leading to a feeling of disempowerment. In addition, gender appeared to exacerbate the difficulties that women teachers faced when attempting to establish their authority (see also Amin, 1999).

In a small-scale study conducted in Hong Kong, Tang (1997) surveyed 47 NNS English teachers about their perceptions of the English proficiency of NS and NNS teachers of English. All the teachers believed that the NS teachers were superior to the NNS teachers in speaking, while 92% believed that the NS teachers were superior in pronunciation, in listening (87%), vocabulary (79%), and reading (72%). Some teachers commented that because NS teachers "provide the need and the opportunity to use English in the classroom setting" (p. 578), students can learn "accurate," "correct," and "natural" English from NS teachers. On the other hand, the teachers stated that their knowledge of the students' mother tongue was advantageous when teaching junior and weak students. Further, their own previous experiences as learners of English was also an advantage.

Because teachers' beliefs and self-perceptions are likely to influence the way they teach, Samimy & Brutt-Griffler (1999) studied 17 NNS graduate students in a TESOL program for their perceptions of NS–NNS issues in English language teaching. Specifically, the aims of the study were to determine how these graduate students perceived themselves as professionals in the field of English language teaching, if they thought there were differences in the teaching behaviors of NS and NNS, what these differences were, and if they felt handicapped as NNS English teachers.

In addition to using a questionnaire similar to that of Medgyes (1994), the researchers also used data from classroom discussions, in-depth interviews with their subjects, and autobiographical accounts written by the subjects. All the subjects were enrolled in a graduate seminar titled "Issues and concerns related to NNS professionals," taught at a large mid-western university in the United States. Their length of stay in the USA ranged from one to four years.

Most had taught English at a university or secondary school, their teaching experience ranging from less than a year to 25 years. In terms of English proficiency, the majority of the subjects claimed to be from average to excellent and the researchers referred to their subjects as a "rather sophisticated group of nonnative speakers of English" (p. 134) who were from Korea, Japan, Turkey, Surinam, China, Togo, Burkina Faso, and Russia.

Responding to the questionnaire, more than two thirds of the subjects admitted that their difficulties with the language affected their teaching from "a little" to "very much." Nearly 90% of the subjects perceived a difference between NS and NNS teachers of English. They identified the former group as being informal, fluent, accurate, using different techniques, methods, and approaches, being flexible, using conversational English, knowing subtleties of the language, using authentic English, providing positive feedback to students, and having communication (not exam preparation) as the goals of their teaching. NNS English teachers were perceived as relying on textbooks, applying differences between the first and second languages, using the first language as a medium of instruction, being aware of negative transfer and psychological aspects of learning, being sensitive to the needs of students, being more efficient, knowing the students' background, and having exam preparation as the goal of their teaching. However, they did not consider the NS teachers superior to their NNS counterparts. During the interviews, the subjects displayed a sense of confidence and self-esteem as English teachers.

Liu (1999) explored the terms "native speaker" and "nonnative speaker" by conducting interviews and discussions with seven NNS who taught English at a large mid-western university in the United States. The respondents were one full-time instructor and six graduate teaching associates in the university's ESL program. The interviews and discussions conducted face-to-face and also through e-mail lasted 16 months. The subjects were originally from Hong Kong, Denmark, Surinam, Zaire, Italy, Korea, and the Philippines. Their first languages were Cantonese, Danish, Dutch, French, Italian, Korean, and Tagalog. One subject had been exposed to English from birth, while the others' exposure had occurred from kindergarten to high school.

In essence, Liu asked the subjects what the label "'nonnative-English-speaking TESOL professional' meant to them and how they defined it based on their own experience" (p. 87). The seven subjects defined the label in various ways. The "simplistic reduction" of a complex phenomenon into a NS–NNS dichotomy was not acceptable to three of the subjects. The others had no difficulty with defining the term or associating themselves with the NNS label. If the label was dependent upon precedence (the order in which languages are learned) or competence in the language, some subjects were prepared to accept the simplistic definition that a NNS would be a person for whom English is not the first language. Other subjects, however, saw the definition as more complex, and favored competence as a defining factor in the NS–NNS dichotomy. Three subjects who had learned English at an early age (and who spoke English without a foreign accent) also had difficulty in labeling themselves as either NS or NNS. None of the subjects would consider their status as NNS or revealing this status as beneficial to their teaching. Discussing his findings on the effects of being a NS or a NNS on language learning and teaching, Liu concludes that it depends on "the sequence in which languages are learned, competence in English, cultural affiliation, self-identification, social environment, and political labeling" (p. 100).

Before the formation of Israel in 1948, English was used as the language of government during British rule from 1914 to 1948. Now, both Hebrew and Arabic are official languages, but Hebrew, being the language of the majority Jewish population, is more widely used. Since 1960, English has been taught as a compulsory subject from Grade 5. The self-perceptions of Israeli NNS English teachers was the focus of a study conducted by Inbar-Lourie (2001), which is probably the first study at doctoral level on NNS issues. The study, conducted in two phases, set out to investigate why some teachers in Israel perceived themselves as NS of English and the effects of the native vs. nonnative distinction on the pedagogical perceptions of the teachers. In the second phase of the study, which is more relevant to the topic of this chapter, the researcher specifically sought to discover if there were differences in perceptions between teachers who claim to be NS of English and those who do not, with regard to the following factors: differences between NS and NNS English teachers; the teaching and status of the English language; English teaching in Israel; and English teaching and assessment methods. Further, Inbar-Lourie also examined the effect of personal and professional background variables on the pedagogical perceptions of the teachers regarding the above issues.

In the first phase, data was gathered through a self-report questionnaire distributed to 102 English teachers in Israel. In the second phase, self-report questionnaires were distributed to 264 English teachers (93 NS and 171 NNS), followed by semi-structured interviews with nine teachers. Results from the first phase indicated that the teachers' NS identity could be explained by nine variables, two of which could best predict this identity: having spoken English from the age of 0 to 6 and others' perception of them as native speakers of English. Results from the second phase of the study indicated that differences between NS and NNS teachers could be detected only in some categories, mainly the superiority of the NS teachers (as espoused by the NS teachers themselves), the degree of confidence in teaching specific language areas, and in student–teacher relations. No differences were found in perception categories relating to teaching and assessment practices, defining students' knowledge of English, the status of the English language, and goals of teaching English. In fact, perception differences in these areas arose not from the teachers' status as NS or NNS but from personal and professional variables such as country of birth, length of residence in the country, school level, and perceived type of school. NNS teachers reported having better relations with students and feeling more confident in using the L1 to facilitate teaching.

Interviews with nine teachers confirmed the results from the self-reports (see also Inbar-Lourie, 2005).

In Australia, despite a preference for NS for English teaching positions, NNS English teachers were recruited from 1948 when an important criterion for teaching English to migrants was the ability to speak Russian, German, or any Baltic or Slavic language (Martin, 1998, cited in Ellis, 2002). In view of Australia's population demographics at that time, these recruits would have been native speakers of these languages, thereby making them NNS of English.

Drawing upon teacher cognition, which examines how teachers' thinking affects their classroom actions, E. Ellis (2002) studied three NNS English teachers in Australia. They were native speakers of (a) a Latin American variety of Spanish; (b) Finnish and Swedish (a bilingual); and (c) Cantonese. Each teacher's class was videotaped for two to three hours and followed up with semi-structured interviews. Using a form of stimulated recall, the subjects were asked about specific episodes from the videotaped lessons in order to explore their philosophies and teaching. The second part of the interviews encouraged the subjects to discuss their personal and professional backgrounds.

Stating that the defining characteristic of NNS English teachers is their experience in learning English as a second language (a characteristic which no NS teacher can claim), Ellis points out that this characteristic is only significant if the experience is accessible and useful to teachers to draw upon during their teaching. She further states that the teachers drew upon their second language learning experience in four ways. The first, affective, factor was manifested in the teachers' empathy with their students' difficulties and frustrations in the classroom. Second, the teachers had direct experience of different teaching and learning styles, and preferred learning styles and strategies. They reflected upon their own teachers in the past and on their own learning and are able to select the "good" and incorporate them into their teaching.

The third manner in which the three teachers drew upon their second-language learning experience was the ability to view the English language from the perspective of NNS. For instance, they have learned the grammar, unlike NS who may have acquired it unconsciously; NS know what "sounds right" but may be unable to explain it in a classroom. According to Ellis, these abilities of NNS come under labels such as "language awareness," "metalinguistic awareness," and "sensitivity to the language." Fourth, the subjects were able to relate what they have learned in TESOL or linguistics (in teacher training courses, for instance) to their own learning of English. If, as commonly acknowledged, teachers' experiences inform their beliefs and, in turn, influence their teaching, and the theories they encounter in teacher training courses reflect their own experiences as language learners, the two blend smoothly in their classroom practices. This ability, to place theory within the context of one's own learning, is not available to NS English teachers.

In Spain, French and English were equally popular languages in secondary schools till the early 1980s. However, by the 1990s French had almost disappeared from the language curriculum. Currently, about 5.5 million students take English in Spanish schools (Antonio Roldán, personal communication). Focusing on one Spanish city, Llurda and Huguet (2003) investigated the self-awareness of 101 nonnative English teachers in primary and secondary schools. Through a set of questions (partially inspired by Medgyes, 1994), administered orally in one-to-one interviews with the teachers, the researchers aimed to determine how these teachers perceived their own language skills, how these skills affected their teaching, and how the skills had evolved over time; the subjects' teaching ideology as expressed through their preferences for designing a language course and their goals as language teachers; and their position in the NS–NNS debate, specifically with regard to the preference for NS or NNS as language teachers and the need for cultural knowledge on the part of English teachers. Only the findings relevant to the topic of this chapter will be discussed here.

In the case of language skills, Llurda & Huguet found that the secondary teachers showed more confidence in their skills than did primary teachers, especially in general proficiency, grammar, knowledge of grammatical rules, and reading comprehension. Although primary teachers admitted that they did experience certain difficulties in teaching English, they did not attribute these difficulties to their proficiency in English. As for language improvement over time, the primary teachers displayed a greater awareness of their language improvement and believed that this improvement came through conscious study of the language.

In the NS or NNS debate, the primary teachers appeared to be more influenced by the native speaker fallacy, half of them stating that they would hire more NS than NNS for a language school, although the other primary teachers did state that they would hire equal numbers of NS and NNS teachers. As for secondary teachers, nearly two thirds chose the balanced option of hiring teachers from both groups. In fact, most of the secondary teachers (65.6%) believed that being a NNS was an advantage.

Unlike in most ELT contexts, the USA draws both English teachers and learners from many countries. Kamhi-Stein, Aagard, Ching, Paik, & Sasser (2004) compared NS and NNS English teachers who taught from kindergarten through Grade 12 in southern California. The 32 NNS teachers who participated in the study were born in Mexico, Taiwan, Korea, El Salvador, and Vietnam. Nearly 90% of them had lived in the US for ten years or more. One segment of the study related to the teachers' self-perceptions of their language skills. The NNS teachers judged their skills as being "very good" or close to that level. For these teachers, listening was the highest self-rated skill, while pronunciation was the lowest rated. In fact, one respondent stated that NNS teachers are sometimes "afraid that they're going to make a mistake when speaking" (p. 91). Vocabulary skills were the second area of difficulty, one respondent stating that inadequate vocabulary knowledge could affect NNS' teaching ability. On the other hand, the multicultural learning environment provided by NNS teachers would "broaden the students' awareness of the world" (p. 92).

Further, these teachers also brought empathy to the classroom because they could better understand the difficulties of second language learning. Finally, many of the teachers at elementary level stated that their "ability to communicate with students' [non-English-speaking] parents promoted parent–teacher rapport" (p. 92).

Jenkins (2005), who has authored several books on English as a lingua franca (ELF), conducted lengthy in-depth interviews with eight NNS English teachers from Italy, Japan, Malaysia, Poland, and Spain. All were university graduates—six also had Master's (degrees)—and were highly proficient in English. The broader aim was to determine the teachers' understanding of ELF and attitudes towards its theory. Some of the interview questions focused on the teachers' attitudes to and identification with NS and NNS English accents, which are relevant to this chapter.

When queried about their attitudes toward their own accents, all the teachers displayed some ambivalence. Three respondents were positive, four were negative or uncertain, and one claimed to have never thought about the matter. When asked about how they would feel if "someone thought your accent was a native-speaker accent" (p. 543), even those who had earlier responded positively to their own (NNS) accents expressed various degrees of attachment to a NS accent. The four respondents who had been negative or uncertain about their accents were more consistent with their views, one saying that she would be "very happy" if hers was considered a NS accent. Another said that she "would be proud of it" and the third said that she would be "flattered." According to another respondent, she "worships" NS pronunciation and claimed that a NS accent would lead her to greater career success. Nevertheless, one of the respondents who had favored a NS accent claimed later in the interview that she was proud of her NNS accent. When asked about a "bad experience" they have had as a result of not being a NS of English, all the respondents cited at least one instance.

In conclusion, Jenkins states that NNS English teachers may "want a NS identity as expressed in a native-like accent" (p. 541). According to the participants in the study, such an accent would be "good," "perfect," "correct," "proficient," "competent," "fluent," "real," and "original English." In their view, a NNS accent would be "not good," "wrong," "incorrect," "not real," "fake," "deficient," and "strong." All the participants had strong attachments to their mother tongues, which in turn may have led to ambivalence and a "love–hate relationship" (Bamgbose, 1998, cited in Jenkins, 2005) with English.

In Greece, English has been taught since 1836 as an optional language in secondary schools. After World War II, English replaced French as the default language in Greek schools and is now compulsory from Grade 3 (Nicos Sifakis, personal communication). Greece's admission to the European Union in 1981 and a large influx of immigrants since has also contributed to the importance of English in Greece. In order to examine Greek English teachers' beliefs about and practices of their English pronunciation, Sifakis & Sougari (2005) surveyed 421 English teachers from primary, lower secondary, and upper secondary state schools. Specifically, the researchers sought teachers' views on pronunciation issues and the links between teaching pronunciation, English as an international language, and the sociocultural identity of NNS speakers of English. All the teachers who participated in the study were university graduates with at least a BA in English language and literature or an equivalent qualification. The questionnaire contained both open- and closed-ended questions.

The results show that all the teachers were "satisfied" with their accents, 50% claiming that they were "very proud" or "extremely proud." As role models in the classroom, they strived to achieve a "good" English accent. The responses from both primary and upper secondary teachers indicated their belief that the norms of English were associated with NS of the language. They were proud of their English because they sounded native-like, were active in language use, and considered themselves NS. Teachers who were less proud of their accents thought they had less exposure to English. On the whole, most of the teachers appeared to be unaware of the concept of English as an international language. Accordingly, NS norms were dominant in Greek teachers' beliefs about English pronunciation.

Following up on her 2002 research, Moussu (2006) conducted a more wide-ranging study on NNS teachers for her doctoral research. She surveyed students, teachers, and administrators of Intensive English Programs (IEP) in the United States. Of the five research questions, the first three referred to student attitudes towards both NS and NNS English teachers, and the results will be summarized in Chapter 4. The fifth question queried administrators of IEPs on their opinions of the teachers, and the results will be summarized in Chapter 7. The focus of the fourth question was the self-perceptions of the teachers, the topic of this chapter.

Specifically, the fourth research question aimed to determine the extent to which the self-perceptions of NS and NNS teachers regarding their teaching compared with the attitudes of their students. Of the 96 ESL teachers who responded to an online questionnaire, only 18 identified themselves as NNS (and this summary will focus on their responses). They came from Argentina, Azerbaijan, Brazil, China, the Czech Republic, Germany, Iceland, Japan, Korea, Reunion Island, Russia, Slovakia, and Somalia.

On the whole, the NNS teachers were less confident of their teaching skills and strengths than their NS counterparts. Even in the case of grammar—normally an area of strength for NNS teachers—the respondents to this survey expressed a low level of accuracy. With regard to the teaching of various skills, NNS teachers showed less confidence in the areas of culture and writing than in teaching reading, grammar, and listening. NNS teachers appeared to be more "comfortable" in teaching intermediate and lower-level classes. As for their strengths, the NNS teachers perceived their shared language learning experience with the students would enable them to relate to the students' difficulties and needs in the classroom. Their foreign accents, lack of self-esteem, and limited knowledge of American culture were perceived as weaknesses. Seven stated that students sometimes made derogatory remarks about NNS teachers.

English has been taught as a compulsory subject in Japanese middle and higher secondary schools since 1890. A large number of English teachers, both expatriate NS and mainly local NNS, teach English at the elementary, primary, secondary, and tertiary level. Since 1987, the government-sponsored Japan Exchange and Teaching (JET) program has recruited foreign nationals to work as assistant language teachers. Although the program costs about US $500 million annually, only about 10% of them had teaching certificates of any kind, let alone English teaching qualifications.

Using three questionnaires, Butler (2007a) surveyed 112 teachers who had "conducted English activities in various forms" (p. 15) in elementary schools in order to determine if the "native speaker fallacy" exists among her subjects. Specifically, the questionnaires sought the subjects to evaluate their own English proficiency, state their perceptions of the short- and long-term goals of English teaching in Japan, and state their attitudes to English language and culture, Japanese language and culture, and English education. Butler states that the majority of her subjects were homeroom teachers, who also taught other subjects and were not trained to teach English. Some elementary schools did have the services of local (Japanese) teachers of English. By 2004, more than 60% of the elementary schools in Japan also had the services of NS English teachers through the JET program or other means. Not surprisingly, about 80% of the respondents to the survey had worked alongside NS English teachers.

About 60% of the subjects supported the statement that English is best taught by NS of the language. A quarter of the subjects neither agreed nor disagreed with the statement while 13% disagreed. The perceptual factors relating to the teachers' beliefs were investigated through an analysis of the teachers' claimed English proficiencies and the short- and long-term goals of English education through statistical analyses of the subjects' responses. When evaluating their own English proficiency, about 85% of the subjects indicated that it did not reach the minimum level needed to conduct English activities. In fact, for all the skills indicated in the questionnaire—listening, oral fluency, oral vocabulary, pronunciation, oral grammar, reading, and writing—the subjects' proficiency was below that of their desired proficiency. Not surprisingly, the subjects who supported the idea that English was best taught at elementary level by NS teachers of English had perceived their English proficiency to be low.

Turkey has a population of 60 million where English is a compulsory school subject. In a wide-ranging study, Dogancay-Aktuna (2008) surveyed 21 teacher educators in Turkey to determine their self-perceptions as NNS. Specifically, the questions relating to self-perceptions asked the subjects to rate their English language skills in comparison with native English speakers, their perceived professional problems, their frequency of interaction with local and foreign TESOL communities, and their perceptions of their own status within the ELT community—whether their NNS status facilitated or hindered them, or if they perceived discrimination. Most subjects had completed their education in Turkey and all had completed graduate degrees in Turkey or abroad. Nearly half the subjects had more than five years' experience in teaching English.

With regard to English proficiency, 41% of the subjects stated that they had no problems with the language. As for areas of improvements, "idiomatic expressions" topped the list, which Dogancay-Aktuna attributes to the majority of subjects having lived only in Turkey. The subjects' place in the NS–NNS continuum did not appear to be clear-cut, many offering "clarifications and stipulations" of their place on the continuum, based sometimes on sociolinguistic aspects of language. Nearly half the subjects claimed their English proficiency to be native- of "near native"-like, while about a third claimed a "not native-like" proficiency.

In evaluating their status as NNS of English, half the subjects claimed that they perceived prejudices against NNS, most of them stating that NS were preferred in Turkey for English teaching positions. However, 43% of the subjects did not consider their NNS status a disadvantage; their considerable professional training and familiarity with the local teaching context were seen as advantageous. The 29% who perceived their NNS as disadvantageous claimed the reasons as the "public's lack of confidence in English language skills" (p. 75) of NNS teachers. As for their NNS status being advantageous professionally, 40% of the subjects cited their understanding of the contexts in which their teacher trainees worked. Another advantage was their understanding of the problems that the teacher trainees would encounter.

Conclusion

What do these studies reveal? First, the range and breadth of the studies are impressive. In little more than a decade, over 1,200 NNS teachers have been surveyed, interviewed, and observed in order to determine their self-perceptions. The research, carried out in both ESL and EFL contexts such as Australia, Britain, Canada, Greece, Hong Kong, Hungary, Israel, Japan, Spain, Turkey, and the USA, involved teachers who were originally from Outer and Expanding Circle countries or territories such as Argentina, Azerbaijan, Brazil, Burkina Faso, China, the Czech Republic, Denmark, El Salvador, Finland, Germany, Hong Kong, Hungary, Iceland, Israel, Italy, Japan, Korea, Malaysia, Mexico, Nigeria, Poland, Reunion Islands, Russia, Slovakia, Somalia, Spain, Surinam, Sweden, Taiwan, Togo, Turkey, Vietnam, Zaire, and Zimbabwe. In terms of first languages, these NNS English teachers spoke Azerbaijani, Chinese (both Mandarin and Cantonese), Czech, Danish, Finnish, regional varieties of French, German, Hebrew, Hungarian, Icelandic, Italian, Japanese, Korean, Malay, regional varieties of varieties of Portuguese, Russian, Vietnamese, and other languages. Some were large-scale studies involving up to 141 teachers; one study involved only three teachers. Most teachers were surveyed through questionnaires. Others were studied intensively through in-depth interviews, classroom discussions, and autobiographical writings.

Strengths of NNS English Teachers

I will first discuss the results of the above studies under the classification of the strengths and shortcomings of the NNS teachers. Earlier in this chapter, I summarized Reves & Medgyes (1994) at some length because theirs is not only the pioneering study in this area; their findings and conclusions have stood the test of time and have been validated by subsequent studies. They found that NNS teachers had "deeper insights into the English language" (p. 361), appeared to be better qualified than their NS counterparts, and showed more empathy towards their students with whom they shared a common first language. Because of their shared linguistic, cultural, and educational backgrounds, these NNS teachers had a better ability to read the minds of their students and predict their difficulties with the English language.

In Samimy & Brutt-Griffler (1999), who studied graduate students at Master's and doctoral level with years of teaching experience, the subjects claimed to be aware of students' negative transfer from their first languages and of the psychological aspects of learning. Further, they were sensitive to the students' needs and had a better awareness of the students' backgrounds. The enhanced understanding of and better relationships with students was echoed by Inbar-Lourie's (2001) subjects in Israel.

The shared linguistic, cultural, and educational backgrounds with students was also an area of strength claimed by the three teachers that E. Ellis (2002) studied. Secondary school English teachers in Spain thought that their NNS status was an advantage (Llurda & Huguet, 2003). The teacher-trainers in Turkey who were the subjects of Dogancay-Aktuna (2008) also claimed not to have any problems with their proficiency in English. Being teacher-trainers, all the subjects had graduate degrees, so this finding is only to be expected.

Shortcomings of NNS English Teachers

Reves & Medgyes (1994) found that the NNS English teachers were "preoccupied" with accuracy and more formal features of English (at the expense of communicative language teaching). About a third of the teachers who responded to their survey admitted to an English proficiency ranging from average to very poor, and 84% to problems with vocabulary or fluency. For nearly 75% of the respondents, these shortcomings in their language proficiency hampered their teaching. In Tang's (1997) study, the NNS English teachers implicitly admitted their lower proficiency in English by overwhelmingly claiming that NS teachers were superior in pronunciation, listening, vocabulary, and reading. The subjects in Samimy & Brutt-Griffler (1999), similar to the teachers surveyed by Reves & Medgyes (1994), admitted that their difficulties with the English language affected their teaching.

Samimy & Brutt-Griffler's (1999) subjects also perceived NNS English teachers as relying on textbooks, which suggests a lack of innovation and creativity in the classroom. These subjects also saw the use of the teachers' and students' mother tongue as the medium of instruction, a practice that is discouraged in current ELT methodology, and preparation for examinations (instead of learning for communication) being the goal of learning in English classes taught by NNS teachers. In Llurda & Huguet (2003), whose study was also influenced by Medgyes (1994), NNS English teachers at the primary level were found to be susceptible to the "native speaker fallacy", while secondary teachers thought that NNS status would be an advantage when teaching English.

Accent appears to be a factor that causes ambiguity in the identity of NNS English teachers. Jenkins' (2005) study of eight teachers is significant because it provides unusually frank insights into the identity of these teachers. All the teachers had undergraduate degrees, six held Master's (degrees) and all had a high proficiency in English. Despite their high level of education, all eight teachers showed a strong preference for a NS accent and a NS identity as well as a sense of inferiority about NNS accents. These findings not only reveal an unusual honesty but also a deep sense of inferiority among the teachers who were studied. Unlike many of the researchers cited so far, Jenkins (2005) is a NS of English and her research method was in-depth interviews, which lasted about an hour with each participant, during which she used prompts that brought up underlying and largely subconscious reasons for the teachers' attitudes. Perhaps the teachers felt freer in opening up with a NS of English. On the other hand, in-depth interviews may also reveal perceptions that remain suppressed. Questionnaires may not be taken seriously by respondents and their responses may be limited by the prompts on the questionnaire. In a study that involved a large number of subjects, half the English teachers in Greece surveyed by Sifakis & Sougari (2005) were satisfied with their accents because they sounded like NS. Moussu (2006) also found that their foreign accents bothered the NNS teachers she surveyed, although identity was not an issue here.

A characteristic of the studies described in this chapter is that most of them have been conducted by NNS. This, no doubt, is an indication of the empowerment of these researchers who are no longer hesitant to acknowledge themselves as NNS, and venture into uncharted territory. On the other hand, research by NNS on issues that are critical to themselves may cast a shadow of doubt on the validity and reliability of the data. It must be pointed out that most of these researchers had not removed themselves, as they should have, from the data gathering process. Instead, some had designed and distributed the questionnaires, conducted interviews, and analyzed the data by themselves. Especially when a NNS researcher asks a NS colleague sensitive questions regarding NNS issues, the frankness of the responses could be open to question.

Chapter 4

Research on Students' Perceptions of NNS English Teachers

The research described in the previous chapter focused on the self-perceptions of NNS English teachers. Research on students' perceptions of these teachers, as crucial as the self-perceptions, if not greater, has a more recent history. One of the first studies in this area was conducted by Moussu (2002) at Brigham Young University in Utah. Moussu's research questions were fourfold: (1) What feelings and expectations did the students have at first when taught by NNS English teachers, and why? (2) What other variables (such as gender, age, first language, etc.) influence the students' perceptions of their NNS teachers at the beginning of the semester? (3) How do the variables of time and exposure to NNS teachers influence the students' perceptions of their teachers?

Moussu's subjects were four NNS English teachers from Japan, Argentina, Ecuador, and Switzerland, and 84 ESL students above the age of 17, both males and females, from 21 different countries. All the students were enrolled in an intensive English program attached to a US university. The students responded to two questionnaires, one given the first day of class, the second given 14 weeks later on the last day of class. Over the 14-week semester, three separate sets of interviews were also conducted with six students. Analysis of the data showed that from the beginning of the semester, the students had positive attitudes towards their NNS teachers. For instance, 68% of the students said that they could learn English just as well from a NNS as from a native speaker, 79% expressed admiration and respect for their NNS teachers, and as many as 84% of the students expected their class with a NNS teacher to be a positive experience. (The Korean and Chinese students, however, expressed negative feelings toward their NNS teachers more frequently than other students.) Time and exposure to the teachers only made the students' opinions more positive by the end of the semester. For instance, to the question, "Would you encourage a friend to take a class with this nonnative English-speaking teacher?" only 56% of the students had answered "yes" at the beginning of the semester. By the end of the semester, 76% had answered "yes" to the same question. (See also Moussu & Braine, 2006).

Liang (2002) also investigated students' attitudes towards NNS English teachers at California State University, Los Angeles. Specifically, the study was designed to investigate 20 ESL students' attitudes towards six ESL teachers' accents and the features of these teachers' speech that contribute to the students' preference for teachers. Five of the teachers were NNS from different language backgrounds and the other was a NS.

The participants listened to brief audio recordings delivered by the six NNS English teachers and rated and ranked the teachers' accents according to a scale of preference. Data was collected through questionnaires, which included information on the participants' background, their beliefs about teaching, and their ranking and preferences. The results showed that, although the participants rated pronunciation/accent in the ESL teachers' speech as very important, pronunciation/accent did not affect the participants' attitudes toward NNS English teachers in their home countries. In fact, they held generally positive attitudes toward these teachers and believed that pronunciation/accent was not as relevant as it appeared in the first place. Further, personal and professional features, as derived from the teachers' speech, such as "being interesting," "being prepared," "being qualified," and "being professional," played a role in the students' preference for teachers. In conclusion, Liang suggests that, instead of focusing on ESL teachers' ethnic and language background, the discussion on NNS English teachers should focus on their level of professionalism.

Kelch & Santana-Willamson (2002) investigated the extent to which teachers' accents contributed to ESL students' attitudes towards NS and NNS English teachers. Their study, carried out at a community college in southern California, involved 56 students at intermediate and high-intermediate levels of English proficiency. Most of the students were Spanish speakers. The others came from Korea and Vietnam.

Students' attitudes towards accents were elicited through audiotapes of recordings made by six female English teachers representing six varieties of English: Standard American, Southern American, British, and English spoken by a Portuguese, a Japanese, and a German speaker. After listening to each speech sample, the students completed a questionnaire to measure their attitudes to the accents. Specifically, the researchers sought to determine if the students could discern NS accents from NNS accents and the advantages of learning English from NS and NNS teachers, as perceived by the students.

The results indicate that the ESL students were not able to differentiate between NS and NNS accents with a high degree of accuracy. The Standard American speaker was judged to be a NS by 70% of the students. However, the Southern American and British speakers were judged to be native by only 39% and 27% of the students respectively. As for the NNS, the Portuguese, Japanese, and German accents were judged native by 40%, 30%, and 5%, respectively, of the responding students. The Portuguese speaker's native rating was second only to that of the Standard American speaker. As for the students' attitudes towards NS and NNS teachers, a direct correlation was seen between what the students' perceived as a NS accent and a higher attitude rating. For instance, a teacher considered a NS was perceived as having a higher level of education and training than a NNS teacher. In terms of teaching for fluency vs. accuracy, and teaching listening, speaking, and pronunciation, the teachers perceived as NS were preferred over NNS teachers.

As for the advantages of NNS English teachers, where the students were responding to two open-ended questions, the "empathy" factor—NNS teachers' better understanding of learning problems and their ability to offer help—were seen as their advantages. These teachers were also seen as sources of motivation for their students. The ability to translate was also seen as an advantage. (The researchers did not solicit students' views on the disadvantages of NS and NNS teachers.)

So far, what has been missing is an investigation of both teachers and students in a single study, and Cheung (2002) filled this need with her research conducted in Hong Kong, where English has been taught for more than 150 years and is one of the official languages. Cheung's objectives were to determine the attitudes of the university students in Hong Kong towards NS and NNS teachers of English, the strengths and weaknesses of these teachers from the perspective of students, and the capability of these teachers in motivating the students to learn English. She also attempted to determine if there was any discrimination against NNS English teachers in Hong Kong.

Cheung triangulated her data collection with the use of questionnaires, interviews, classroom observations, and post-classroom interviews. The questionnaire was distributed to 420 randomly selected undergraduates from a variety of majors at seven universities in Hong Kong. Most of the participants (98%) were Cantonese or Putonghua speakers, and 99% of them had learned English either in Hong Kong or in China. Ten students from three universities were also interviewed.

On the whole, the Hong Kong university students surveyed for this study showed a positive attitude towards NNS English teachers. During the survey, most students reported that they did not encounter problems with these teachers because of their non-nativeness. They stated that NNS teachers taught as effectively as NS teachers and had no difficulty in understanding and answering students' questions. They believed that the NNS teachers made a sincere effort to communicate with their students, and, simply stated, they liked studying with NNS teachers. During the interviews, students elaborated on the reasons for their positive attitudes, stating that NNS teachers could apply effective strategies in teaching English as they had gone through a similar educational system, shared the same cultural background, and therefore understood the difficulties faced by local students. Local NNS English teachers could make use of Cantonese, the students' first language, in explaining difficulties encountered in English classes. They were capable of designing teaching materials according to the needs and learning styles of the students. A noteworthy result of the study is that students' positive attitudes towards NNS English teachers tended to increase with longer stay at the university: third- (final) year students indicated a more positive attitude than first- and second-year students. The students also voiced their concerns regarding the shortcomings of NNS English teachers. They remembered being spoon-fed English lessons in primary schools and an over-emphasis on past exam papers in secondary school English classes. Their NNS teachers also over-corrected their mistakes in English usage. But the majority of students in this study said that they would rather learn from local NNS English teachers instead of NS teachers with more prestigious accents (see also Cheung & Braine, 2007).

In the Basque Autonomous Community, which is one of the 17 such communities in Spain, English is taught at primary, secondary, and university levels mainly by NNS English teachers. Lasagabaster & Sierra (2002) surveyed 76 undergraduates in the Basque region to determine their perceptions of NS and NNS teachers. The researchers classified the students into two groups, one consisting of English majors and the other of Basque, Spanish, and German majors, under "Other Philologies", for the study. The students were also classified into subgroups depending on their previous experience with NS English teachers. The students completed a Likert scale questionnaire which sought their preferences for NS and NNS teachers at primary, secondary, and university level, specifically in relation to language skills, grammar, vocabulary, pronunciation, learning strategies, culture and civilization, attitudes, and assessment.

In general, the students preferred NS English teachers and this was especially evident among those who had been taught by NS teachers. NS teachers were also preferred at all educational levels—primary, secondary, and university— with an increased preference for NS teachers as the educational level rose. This trend was also stronger among English majors and those who had been taught by NS teachers. In language skill areas—pronunciation, speaking, vocabulary— and culture and civilization, the preference for NS was stronger than for NNS teachers. In assessment, too, the preference was for NS teachers, especially among the English majors. On the other hand, NNS were preferred in teaching strategies and in grammar. Discussing their results, the researchers point out that the English majors may have been influenced by a more integrative goal toward the English language when stating their perceptions.

The first doctoral research into students' perceptions was conducted by Ahmar Mahboob (2003) at the Indiana University in Bloomington, USA. Mahboob's study was conducted in two phases, and the second phase of the study is more relevant to this chapter because it examines students' perceptions of NNS teachers. Instead of using questionnaires to survey the students, Mahboob used the novel and more insightful "discourse-analytic" technique, asking 32 students enrolled in an intensive English program to provide written responses to a cue[1] that solicited their opinions on NS and NNS language teachers. The student essays were coded individually by four readers who, in turn, classified the students' comments according to linguistic factors (oral skills, literacy skills, grammar, vocabulary, culture), teaching styles (ability to answer questions, teaching methodology), and personal factors (experience as an ESL learner, hard work, affect). The analysis of these comments showed that both NS and NNS teachers received positive and negative comments. In the case of NS teachers, the majority of positive comments related to oral skills, with vocabulary and culture also being viewed positively. Negative comments on NS teachers related to grammar, experience as an ESL learner, ability to answer questions, and methodology. In the case of NNS teachers, experience as an ESL learner earned the highest number of positive comments, followed by grammar, affect, oral skills, methodology, hard work, vocabulary, culture, ability to answer questions, and literacy skills. The students also saw NNS teachers as more understanding and empathetic. Generally, NNS were seen as capable teachers except in the teaching of speaking and pronunciation. Mahboob concludes that ESL students in the USA do not have a clear preference for either NS or NNS English teachers. In the students' opinion, both types of teachers have their own strengths and unique attributes. (See also Mahboob, 2004.)

Since his pioneering work on NNS English teachers in 1994, Medgyes has continued to study these teachers' self-perceptions, first in Reves and Medgyes (1994) and ten years later in Benke & Medgyes (2005). The latter study aimed to determine the most characteristic features of both NS and NNS teachers as seen by students, the aspects of teaching behavior where the differences are most apparent, and the extent to which the differences in NS and NNS teachers, as viewed by the teachers themselves, are in accordance with students' perceptions.

The respondents were 422 Hungarian students of English who were selected on the basis of their exposure to both NS and NNS English teachers for a minimum of one year, and a minimum level (lower-intermediate) of English proficiency. The respondents, two-thirds of whom were secondary school students, were surveyed through a questionnaire that contained five parts based on Likert scales as well as open-ended questions.

In their attitudes and opinions regarding NNS teachers, 77%, 74%, and 66%, respectively, of the students stated that these teachers would often or always assign a lot of homework, thoroughly plan their lessons, and check for errors consistently. Further, 76% of the students stated that the NNS teachers rarely or never lost their patience and tended to use eclectic teaching methods (63%). When compared with their NS counterparts, the advantages most often attributed to NNS teachers were their ability to teach grammar in a more structured manner and the ability to handle grammar problems. Because they had a better knowledge of the local educational system, NNS teachers can better prepare students for local examinations. Because they are on the same "wavelength" as local students, these NNS are able to promote language learning more effectively. In addition, they can provide exact Hungarian equivalents of English lexical items. On the negative side, the NNS tend to use more Hungarian in English classes, and were also criticized for poor pronunciation and the use of outdated language forms.

Following up on her 2002 research, summarized previously in this chapter, Moussu (2006) conducted a more wide-ranging study on NNS teachers for her doctoral research. She surveyed students, teachers, and administrators of Intensive English Programs (IEP) in the United States. Of the five research questions, the first three referred to students' attitudes towards both NS and NNS English teachers. Specifically, the initial attitudes of the students towards NS and NNS English teachers and the effects of time and exposure on their attitudes were measured. Students were surveyed twice, at the beginning and at the end of a semester. For this discussion, only the attitudes towards NNS teachers will be considered.

The student questionnaire was divided into two sections, the first on the students' current teachers consisting of both multiple-choice questions and statements that were to be ranked on a Likert scale. The second part of the questionnaire contained multiple-choice questions and short-answer questions about the students' demographics, their reasons for learning English, the number of their previous NS and NNS English teachers, their' intentions to return to their home countries, and the grades they expected to obtain in their current ESL courses.

The initial questionnaire received responses from 804 students and the final questionnaire from 643 students. They came from ten language backgrounds, with Korean, Spanish, Japanese, and Chinese represented by over 100 students each. Overall, the students began with a positive attitude towards their NNS teachers at the beginning of the semester, 79% of them stating that they would encourage a friend to enroll in a class taught by their NNS teacher. In addition, 87% of these students (who were taking classes with a NNS teacher), agreed that their teacher was a "good teacher." Moussu speculates that the students may have been "reevaluating" the negative beliefs they had about NNS teachers after being taught by them.

Variables such as the students' first language, class subject (the language skill area that was the focus of their class), level of English proficiency, expected grade for the course, and the teachers' country of origin also affected their attitudes. Asian students, particularly those from Korea, had the most negative attitude towards NNS teachers. On the other hand, students from Spanish, French, and Portuguese language backgrounds had more positive attitudes. In terms of the language skill areas being taught, students did not appear to be as satisfied as expected with the NNS teachers who taught grammar, despite grammar teaching being generally considered an area of strength for NNS teachers. Students at a higher level of English proficiency showed a more positive attitude towards NNS teachers. Students' attitudes also differed significantly based on the teachers' country of origin.

Considering that the students were surveyed at the beginning and end of the semester, the influence of time was an important focus of Moussu's study. A comparison of the responses to the two questionnaires showed that students who were taught by NNS teachers displayed a more positive attitude towards their teachers at the end of the semester. Although only 32% of the students responded positively with regard to their NNS teachers' accents at the beginning of the semester, it increased to 45% by the semester's end. Further, the percentage of students who strongly agreed to the statement that they could learn English equally well from NS and NNS teachers rose from 29% at the beginning of the semester to 42% at the end.

In South Korea, English is taught in elementary schools from Grades 3 to 6. All elementary-level teachers are Koreans, although many elementary students are believed to be taking lessons from private tutors who are NS of English. Using a matched-guides technique, Butler (2007b) examined the effects of Korean elementary school teachers' accents on their students' listening comprehension. The participants were 312 Grade 6 students enrolled in two public schools, one in the capital, Seoul, and the other in an industrial city where few foreigners or English signs were to be seen.

The participating students performed three tasks. In a comprehension test, they listened to a tape recording of oral material, either in American-accented or Korean-accented English (both recordings were made by the same speaker, a Korean-American), followed by a series of comprehension questions to which the participating students responded. They also responded to questions that measured their attitudes to the "two" speakers. Second, the participants listened to both recordings and, once again, responded to questions that measured their attitudes to the speakers. In the third task the participants were asked about their experiences with NS of English.

Butler concluded that the accents did not affect the participants' listening comprehension to a significant degree. In the case of students' attitudes, some significant differences were found. The American-accented speaker was regarded as having a better pronunciation and more confidence in the use of English, and likely to focus more on fluency and use less Korean in class. The participating students showed a stronger preference for the American-accented speaker as their English teacher. Further analysis of the results showed that the students with high scores in the comprehension test had more confidence in both accents.

Conclusion

As with the studies of NNS teachers' self-perceptions, many of the studies summarized in this chapter had been conducted in the USA: Moussu, 2002; Liang, 2002; Kelch & Santana-Williamson, 2002; Mahboob, 2003; and Moussu, 2006. The three studies conducted in EFL contexts were by Cheung (2002), Benke & Medgyes (2005), and Butler (2007b), in Hong Kong, Hungary, and Korea respectively. In all, the views of over 2,000 students in middle schools, intensive English programs, and universities were sought.

Nevertheless, the studies on students' perceptions were fewer than those on teachers' self-perceptions. This could be partly attributed to the fact that not all students taught by NNS teachers are in a position to evaluate the teachers because there is no basis for comparison. In the Inner Circle (that is, in ESL contexts), most students have the opportunity to learn from both NS and NNS English teachers. But, in the Expanding Circle (where the context is EFL), this opportunity does not always exist. For instance, Cheung (2002), Benke & Medgyes (2005), and Butler (2007b) were able to conduct their studies in Hong Kong, Hungary, and Korea, respectively, because, in addition to local NNS teachers, expatriate NS teachers are also present in large numbers in these contexts. Similar studies of students' perceptions would not be possible in India and Sri Lanka, for instance, because few NS English teachers are employed there. The vast majority of students are taught by local English teachers.

When discussing research on students' perceptions, two studies that figure prominently are those conducted by Moussu (2002, 2006). Although data was gathered through questionnaires, Moussu surveyed a large number of students. Perhaps the most striking result that emerges from her studies is that the students' generally positive attitudes towards NNS increased after being taught by these teachers. Another finding of both studies is the consistently negative attitude towards NNS teachers expressed by Asian students, particularly those from Korea. This is a phenomenon that merits further investigation.

The Kelch & Santana-Williamson (2002) study, which investigated the recognition of NS and NNS English accents by students, is significant in view of the study by Jenkins (2005) presented in Chapter 3. Jenkins, who interviewed eight highly qualified and proficient NNS English teachers, found that the teachers not only lacked confidence in their own accents but also greatly admired NS accents. Kelch & Santana-Williamson's findings, which showed that a sample of ESL could not even differentiate between NS and NNS accents with a high degree of accuracy, should therefore allay the fears of NNS teachers about their accents.

Readers familiar with ELT in Hong Kong and the heavy criticism leveled at local NNS English teachers may be surprised by the results of Cheung's (2002) study, in which a cross-section of university students displayed a generally positive attitude towards NNS. The students' attitudes could be due to a number of reasons. Most students, having been taught by both NS and NNS teachers, probably realize that a well-qualified local English teacher who is familiar with the local language and culture is as good as any NS English teacher. Another reason could be the students' exposure to more NS teachers. In government primary and secondary schools, the only NS teachers are English teachers, whereas at the tertiary level students are likely to meet such teachers in many other disciplines as well. They are also likely to hear more native-speaker accents, some of them difficult to comprehend, and realize that English spoken with a Cantonese accent is probably easier to deal with and is more appropriate for the Hong Kong context.

Although they are useful for collecting data from large groups of subjects, questionnaires are not the most reliable instruments for data collection.

A welcome change from the use of questionnaires was seen in Mahboob's (2003) study, which asked students to provide written responses to a cue that sought their responses to NS and NNS English teachers. Another problematic area in the study of students' perceptions is how students define NS and NNS. Anecdotal evidence suggests that, from some students' viewpoints, all Caucasians (including Finns, Germans, Russians, and Swedes, for instance) are NS of English. Other students, especially Asian-Americans, may not consider American-born Asians to be native speakers of English simply because they are not Caucasian. Hence, when pilot testing questionnaires for use in survey research, or when planning interviews, researchers should ensure that their student informants have a reasonable understanding of the terms "NS" and "NNS."

Chapter 5

An English Teacher from the Outer Circle

Ultimately, the future of the NNS movement depends on individual English teachers, whether in ESL or EFL contexts, irrespective of their presence in the Inner, Outer, or Expanding circles, or in affluent or impoverished countries. In millions of classrooms around the world, English teachers and learners of English, perhaps numbering more than a billion, are engaged in teaching and learning English every day. However, little is known about these NNS teachers—their socioeconomic backgrounds, levels of education and training, day-to-day association with the English language, or if they teach English more as a means of livelihood than as a calling. Some personal narratives have appeared in magazines, academic journals, and in *Teaching English to the World* (Braine, 2005). Nevertheless, Medgyes' (2000) statement that, "on the whole, the study of the non-native teacher remains a largely unexplored area in language education" (p. 445), still remains true. Hence, in this chapter and the next I will explore closely the lives of two NNS English teachers, one who was born in Malaysia, from the Outer Circle, and the second from China, in the Expanding Circle.

Malaysia is located in Southeast Asia and has a landmass of 329,847 square kilometres and a population of about 27 million. The country is separated into two regions—Peninsular Malaysia and Malaysian Borneo—by the South China Sea. Malaysia as a unified state came into being only in 1963. Previously, Britain had established a set of colonies, starting from 1786, that came to be known as British Malaya: which in turn became the Federation of Malaya. Independence was gained in 1957. In 1963, Singapore, Sarawak, British North Borneo and the Federation of Malaya joined to form Malaysia, which Singapore left two years later. The majority of the population consists of Malays. Bahasa Malaysia is the official language with Islam the official religion. Substantial numbers of Chinese and Indians also live in Malaysia, forming 26% and 8% of the population respectively. With a GDP of nearly US$15,000, Malaysia is one of the wealthier countries in Asia.

In Malaysia, the education system is highly centralized and primary and secondary education in government schools is handled by the Ministry of Education. State and local governments have little say in the curriculum or other major aspects of education. Standardized tests are a common feature. The language of instruction in government schools is Malay, which replaced English as the medium of education in mainstream schools from the 1970s. In 2003, the government reintroduced the use of English as a medium of instruction in all science subjects, but the policy has been difficult to implement because of the low English proficiency of many teachers.

Maria's Story

Maria (a pseudonym) was born in the late 1940s in what was called Malaya at that time, in Johor Bahru, a small town with two main streets and separated from Singapore by a three-quarter-mile stretch of water.[1] Her parents had immigrated to Malaya from China, her father from Fujian and her mother from Kwangtung/Canton. He spoke a Hokkien/Fujian dialect and she spoke Cantonese. Maria says that her parents were "part of the streams of Chinese from southern China who left poverty in their homeland for British Singapore/ Malaya hoping to make a fortune and return to 'Sugar Mountain' [as they called their homeland] to live in comfort." However, many of these immigrants never returned to China, instead staying back in Malaya and Singapore to become citizens.

Maria's father was a carpenter who also undertook small contract jobs. Although they weren't very poor—Malaya's economy, due to its rubber production, boomed during the Korean War—Maria says her father never became rich. They did not own a radio in those early years and TV came to Malaya only when Maria was in Primary Six; but even then, few homes could afford it. In today's politically correct terms, Maria calls her mother a "homemaker" who did all the housework and shopping. She also taught Maria to read the Chinese calendar and Cantonese nursery rhymes. Maria says that she still reads the Chinese calendar with a Cantonese internal voice.

When she was growing up in Malaya, English was the language of the Tuan, a Malay term meaning "Sir," which was used to refer to the British who occupied all the positions of power in government and commerce. Because Malaya was a British colony, English was the language of government and the medium of instruction in English schools. However, Maria's world consisted of Hokkien and Cantonese spoken at home and Hainanese spoken by her neighbors across the stream running beside her house. These neighbors used Cantonese when conversing with Maria's family. Maria says she heard "enough Hainanese to learn the insults." Malays also lived in the neighborhood but Maria didn't learn Malay because her house was too far from Malay homes for children to get together.

Maria's first encounter with English occurred on her first day at school. She was six years old and didn't know "a word of English" because there had been no preschools or kindergartens in Johor Bahru for the non-English-speaking poor people. So Maria didn't understand what the teacher was saying. Miss Kuok, the teacher, didn't (or may not have been allowed to) speak Cantonese or Hokkien. Nevertheless, Maria does not recall feeling traumatized or frightened, possibly because she was "too young and inexperienced to be able to verbalize any feeling of trauma" or because she was in the same boat as the majority of the other children in class. Although they came from various language backgrounds—different Chinese dialects, Malay, Tamil, Malayalam—only a handful perhaps were familiar with English.

Early Education

The primary school Maria attended was called the Convent of the Holy Infant Jesus and was run by nuns from Ireland and France. She remembers a large room (a hall) where the students assembled every morning to sing a hymn and say prayers in English. The same hall was used for lessons in music and movement by a Ms. Aishah Akbar, who played the piano and taught the children to sing and move to music.

The most important subjects taught were English and arithmetic. The teacher of the Primary One class had pictures propped up on an easel to teach the children their first English words. Early morning, before the commencement of the regular timetable, there was catechism class for Catholic students. During the catechism class, non-Catholic students had to stay in class with a teacher. As Maria was not too keen on the substitute teacher, she opted to join the catechism class and learn to recite prayers and church precepts from a little red catechism, "thus beginning a decade's journey into the Catholic Church."

The teachers in primary school were foreign nuns and local teachers. Now, from the perspective of an English teacher educator, Maria says that her teachers spoke perfect English. At that time, there was no Malaysian English; one either spoke English or one didn't. Maria doesn't remember noticing a difference between the English spoken by the European nuns and the local teachers, including some nuns. They were all fluent. English was a second language for most of the foreign nuns too, since they were mainly Irish or French.

Junior and Secondary Education

For her junior and secondary education, too, Maria attended the same school, the Convent of the Holy Infant Jesus, since, at the time, primary, junior and secondary school were one school. English, mathematics, science, history, and geography were the core subjects taught. They were taught by local teachers and the foreign nuns, all fluent in English. The textbooks were both locally produced and imported from Britain. The local textbook industry was in its infancy but English and content subject books were produced by a local branch of reputable publisher, Oxford University Press.

The imported books were about life in England and other parts of the world, such as India, Europe, Africa, and the USA, and the contents ranged from descriptions of everyday life to factual information. Classics of English literature, such as *Great Expectations, Pride and Prejudice,* and *Little Women,* were first read in simplified versions in lower secondary and later in their full-length version. The English curriculum in upper primary and secondary school included lessons on nouns, verbs, and other grammatical parts of speech. Maria remembers having to identify dependent/independent clauses and subject/object in sentences, and a textbook "with a red cover and low quality paper from India" that contained written exercises on grammar.

Maria had English lessons every day of the week, about five hours per week. But English was reinforced in all the classes because all subjects were taught in English. Every teacher was fluent in English, including the teachers who taught Malay. As for accent, Maria says that the teachers didn't sound English or American. They spoke standard, correct English.

In English classes, teachers didn't use grammar translation because students were not allowed to speak their home language in class. Because the students came from multiethnic and multilingual backgrounds without a shared language, there wasn't one common language that teacher and all students could use. Instead, teachers used only English to teach English. Maria spoke English in school and outside school when interacting with school friends. All the extracurricular activities—such as the literary society, the debating society, and the Young Christian Students Society—were conducted in English.

Throughout their primary and secondary education, students were advised to read a lot in English, and many did. Maria says she read "copiously," simply anything she could lay her hands on. She borrowed storybooks from better-off classmates and read old newspapers used to wrap provisions her mother bought. Once she learned to read, Maria was in love with print. In some ways, it was fortunate that TV hadn't then arrived in Malaya.

In primary school, Maria remembers "devouring" Enid Blyton. Later, in secondary school, there were the books about the Scarlet Pimpernel, books by G. K. Chesterton, classics like *Silas Marner,* American authors like Zane Grey, and tearjerkers like *How Green was My Valley.* Because it was a convent school, books on the lives of saints were also available. Maria also read non-fiction and says that Thor Heyerdahl's *Kon-Tiki Expedition* made a lasting impression on her.

Maria remembers listening to the pop songs that wafted over from the neighbor's radio. There was no radio at home and her parents couldn't afford a TV when television arrived in Malaya in the early 1960s. She does remember watching some programs in the home of her tuition teacher. Maria remarked that her parents preferred to spend on tuition instead of buying a radio because they greatly valued education.

Maria says that the learning of English was neither interesting nor boring. At that time, many students simply accepted school and homework, and sat obediently through lessons. She didn't find English difficult and remembers being amazed at getting praised for her English compositions. Looking back, she wonders where it all came from, herself as a child of immigrant non-English parents with these English words pouring effortlessly out of her.

English literature was a separate subject. At the General Certificate of Education (Ordinary Level) classes, the texts were *As You Like It*, *The Tempest*, Gerald Durrell's *My Family and other Animals*, and a book written by a British colonial officer about his experiences on a Pacific island. At the Advance Level, Maria studied more Shakespeare, including his sonnets, the Romantics Keats and Wordsworth, and Victorian or 18th century novels.

Higher Education

At the age of 19, Maria entered the University of Malaya in Kuala Lumpur. She was 300 miles from Johor Bahru, away from home for the first time. The curriculum was modeled on those of the British universities of that time, the late 1960s. One unusual feature was that an honours degree could be obtained at the end of the third year for those who did well. In her first year, Maria read literature, history (both taught in English), and Malay Studies (taught in Malay). Since a foreign language was compulsory, she took French. In the second and third years, she specialized in English literature. She spoke only English both in and out of class.

Maria recalls the university setting, with a lake and a drive leading from the main road, as beautiful. It was green and serene. (She recently returned to the university after an absence of 35 years and feels that it has been overbuilt.) The library was well stocked and had all the books for her undergraduate studies. The academic staff was a mix of local and expatriate teachers. There was a dramatic Shakespeare lecturer, Edward Dorall, who was Eurasian, and local and British lecturers Mr. and Mrs. Price who taught Chaucer and the Elizabethan playwrights. Another teacher was the pipe-smoking Dr. Christopher Ward, who "bedazzled [the students'] half-comprehending minds with his learning on T.S. Eliot." Two lecturers from other British Commonwealth countries were Dr. Kazmi, a Pakistani who taught the Victorian novel, and Prof. Lloyd Fernando from Sri Lanka, who was head of the English department. Some years ago, Maria was reminded of her university lecturers and tutors when she read Shirley Lim's *Among the White Moon Faces*. Lim had been a tutor in the English Department when Maria was an undergraduate.

As for extracurricular activities, she participated in plays, poetry readings, and talks of the Literary and Drama Society. She also supported the Society in soliciting advertisements from businesses around Kuala Lumpur and in putting up posters advertising plays. For a time, she also reported for the campus newspaper.

Maria read widely beyond the required English texts: novels, self-help books, magazines, newspapers. She says that the worlds she entered through these books were interesting and fascinating: "The worlds were so varied—the American frontier in books like the *Grapes of Wrath*, the genteel world of

Jane Austen's characters, the angst and ideals of Keats and the other romantics, and the familiar and yet so different life in other British colonies depicted in novels like *A House for Mr. Biswas*." She says that the word "boring" never occurred to her, although literature may have been challenging because of the looming deadlines for the many papers she had to write.

Teaching Career

According to Maria, one reason for her choosing a teaching career was the view that prevailed in the 1960s, that teaching was a "suitable" job for women who were expected to marry and have children before they were 30. Because teachers were at school from 7.30 in the morning till 1.30 in the afternoon, they could be home by 2 pm to take care of the family. Another reason was that the Convent of the Holy Infant Jesus had sponsored her university education in the expectation that she would return to the Convent as a teacher. However, by the time she graduated from the university, the Malaysian Ministry of Education regulated that the state education department should handle all teaching appointments and postings. So she could not return to the convent school and was posted to a boys' school instead. As a result, during the first few years of her working life, Maria paid back to the convent the interest-free loan she had received for her university education. She later learned that these funds had sponsored a Vietnamese refugee's studies in France.

Maria was posted to St. Joseph's Secondary School, which had been founded by an order of Catholic brothers known as the Brothers of St. Gabriel. This school was also in Johor Bahru, which in the 1960s was still a sleepy town with no shopping malls, no high-rise complexes, no 5- or 4-star hotels, and no traffic jams. Local residents were either in business or worked for the government. The British military had a presence in the area, so a cluster of businesses served the needs of British servicemen—rental housing, provision stores delivering food and provisions to British families, and employment in British homes as cooks and domestic help.

St. Joseph's did not have modern facilities, not even fans in the classrooms, but it had a playing field, science labs, and a library with English books. At the beginning, Maria taught English language and literature to boys in Form 4 and 5 classes. English was the medium of instruction in all schools in Malaysia[2] at the time. Her students came from a variety of socioeconomic backgrounds: some were sons of businessmen and professionals, while others were the sons of technicians, shop assistants, and manual workers. The students paid school fees, a nominal amount of about M$8. The fees were low because the school was funded by government grants.

At that time, students in Malaysia, similar to those in other British Commonwealth countries, were required to take the General Certificate of Education (Ordinary Level) examination conducted by Cambridge University. In English classes, students were occupied with summary writing, answering comprehension questions based on their readings, and compositions of the narrative, descriptive and expository genres. Although she cannot recall the titles of the English textbooks used at that time, she remembers that the authors' names were Etherton, Heaton, and L.G. Alexander. The textbooks were more functional than attractive. There may not have been pictures and they were in black and white because the use of color would have driven the price up. Maria also taught English literature and she remembers teaching *Julius Caesar* (the original text, not a simplified version) and Wordsworth's poetry. A student from her first year at St. Joseph's Secondary School, who is now the CEO of a large hospital in Singapore, had mentioned to one of Maria's colleagues recently that she was the "best literature teacher" he ever had. He remembered the *Julius Caesar* lessons in particular. Maria says her enthusiasm for Shakespeare must have made up for her lack of expertise in the classroom. In the 1970s in Malaysia, the belief was that a degree in English literature qualified a person to teach both English literature and language.

In accordance with prevailing practices of that era, the classrooms were traditional and teacher-centered. The teacher would set the exercises and composition topics and would then go through the students' work with a red pen, circling and underlining all the mistakes. Maria first heard the term "audiolingual" when she enrolled at the Regional English Language Centre (RELC) in Singapore in 1973 to study for the Diploma in TESL/TEFL (later to be known as Diploma in Applied Linguistics).

After a year at St. Joseph's, Maria was transferred by the State Education Department to Temonggong Ibrahim Teachers' College in the same town, Johor Bahru. The Teachers' College trained teachers for lower secondary schools and Maria taught courses in English language proficiency, language teaching methodology, and language study (linguistics). The students had applied to the Ministry of Education to join the teaching service and came from all over Malaysia.

Maria taught at the Teachers' College for 12 years. As the years progressed, she noted that more and more students came from rural areas, were predominantly Malay (due the government's New Economic Policy to improve the economic status of Malay citizens), and were not as proficient in English as students in her first few years at the College. English was a compulsory subject for all teacher trainees (irrespective of their majors), and for some of the trainees, it was really a foreign language. As a result, English language classes were purely proficiency classes. Simplified readers had to be used, such as the simplified stories of Rabindranath Tagore.

Maria remembers that, in the case of English teacher trainees, the standard of English was a little higher as the students tended to be from more urban areas. But, with these students, too, her dilemma was "whether to spend the limited curriculum time upgrading the students' language proficiency or teaching them linguistics and language teaching methodology." For linguistics, the library had reference books which Maria used in the preparation of her lectures and which students were advised to consult. For pronunciation, the reference book was Daniel Jones' *The Pronunciation of English* and for language teaching methodology it was Wilga Rivers' *Teaching Foreign Language Skills*. In fact, the library had a good supply of English books—on literature, science, art, history, and other subjects. These were books accumulated during the years when English was the medium of instruction in Malaysian schools, colleges, and universities.

Although the teaching method in vogue in the 1970s was audiolingual, it wasn't appropriate for the teacher trainees who were in their early to late twenties. Because getting these young adults to repeat English sentences mindlessly was dreary for both teacher and students, Maria combined audiolingual teaching with explicit teaching of grammar. In some of the classes, she had to explain the grammar in Malay because the students' English proficiency was not enough for them to understand explanations in English.

For leisure reading, Maria had newspapers, *Time* and *Newsweek*. English reading materials were freely available in libraries and local bookshops. She only watched English programs on TV as these were the only programs that appealed to her, although Malaysian TV also had programs in Malay, Chinese, and Tamil.

Teacher Training

On graduating with a BA honors degree from the University of Malaya, Maria obtained a Diploma in Education (now known as PGDE—Postgraduate Diploma in Education) from the Teachers' Training College in Singapore, which is now known as the National Institute of Education. Singapore was only a short drive across a narrow strip of water from Johor Bahru, where Maria taught and lived. The course was part-time, taught in the afternoons and on Saturday mornings. Maria, along with a few other teachers, would drive over to Singapore in two cars to attend classes. The Teachers' Training College was on Paterson Road during those days, off fashionable Orchard Road and within walking distance of the Lido Theatre and all the grand shops. But Maria had no time to shop or for the theatre because they arrived just in time for the lectures and hurried home afterwards, to attend to family responsibilities and to prepare for the next day's teaching.

The diploma course lasted one academic year and included courses in educational psychology, sociology of education, philosophy of education, and health education taught by a medical doctor. All the subjects were taught in English. Maria says that, for the first time in her life, she discovered that "pronunciation is a subject that is a course by itself." She was "fascinated" by the IPA symbols and by the fact that there are names for the different sounds. Apart from the pronunciation course, which she enjoyed, there wasn't much to learn from the course on ESL teaching methodology. English was regarded as a first language and taught as such.

All teachers in Malaysian schools are required to have professional training, which at the time was the Diploma in Education for graduate teachers. Without the diploma, a teacher couldn't be made permanent in a teaching position and be placed on the salary scale for graduate teachers.

Attitudes and Perceptions

Having been an English language teacher for nearly 40 years, Maria has become more reflective and more confident of her pedagogical skills. A sense of detachment gives her the opportunity to view both teaching and research outcomes in a more scientific manner with less inclination to blame and more readiness to explore.

As far as balancing work, study, and family are concerned, Maria says she still takes students' papers home to grade despite spending 10 to 12 hours a day in her office. She can commit these long hours to work because she does not have growing children at home. Nevertheless, she'll leave early to have dinner with family or friends or to attend a concert. She also makes it a point not to think about work issues when she leaves the office.

In Maria's family, the language of communication is English. She says the reasons are historical. When she was starting school in Malaya, the best public/government schools were in the English medium. Her parents, realizing that an English medium education was the path to economic success, sent her to such schools. As a result, as she became more and more immersed in English, Cantonese—the native language—became restricted to the spoken domain at home. She says that her husband, who is of Sri Lankan Tamil ancestry, experienced a similar situation. English was and is their only common language.

For Malaysians, English has become the dominant language in homes where the parents had completed schooling before the late 1970s, before the medium of instruction changed to Malay. In Singapore (where Maria resides now), the medium of instruction has remained English. As a result, an increasing number of children entering school are from homes where English is the only language of communication or is one of the regularly used languages.

Comparing the teaching of English and the current generation of English teachers in Malaysia and Singapore, Maria sees sharp differences. The current generation of English teachers in Malaysia were schooled in a system that had downgraded English in the interest of nationalism. Thus, when the former Prime Minister Dr. Mahathir Mohammad realized that the country's advancement in science and technology had slowed as a result of the Malaysians' poor English skills, he ordered the reinstatement of English as the medium of instruction in science and mathematics. However, the teachers of these subjects had graduated from schools where English was of little importance, and many could barely teach in English. Here, Maria narrates an anecdote about her niece who attended school in Malaysia's capital, Kuala Lumpur, whose science teacher would close the door of her classroom so that only her students would hear her ungrammatical English!

Maria says that many English teachers in Malaysia are probably using Malay to provide explanations and to manage classroom activities. In the late 1970s and early 1980s, when Maria taught at a training college for secondary school teachers, she observed that the teacher trainees in each year's intake were becoming less and less proficient in English. Although the situation in Malaysia and Singapore were similar 40 years ago, Singapore continued with English as the medium of instruction while Malaysia abandoned it. The result is that Singapore has enough polytechnic and university graduates who are proficient in English and can teach the language with confidence. In addition, an English teacher's job in Singapore is far easier than that of a Malaysian counterpart because Singaporean students are surrounded by English, through English newspapers and magazines, radio and TV programs, advertisements on buses, billboards, at train stations, public notices in shops and government buildings, and in lessons and other school activities throughout the day. For many students, English has become the language for social interaction. However, this might be a mixed blessing because, increasingly, students are unable to distinguish between Singlish and standard English. In fact, they even expect foreigners visiting Singapore for the first time to understand Singlish.

In Hong Kong, another former British colony, the general impression is that the English standard of students is on the decline. The blame falls mainly on local English teachers. Maria says this impression prevails in Singapore too, although she does not blame English teachers for the decline. Although not all English teachers in Singapore speak standard English, Maria says the use of English has now spread into mobile phones, texting, and other non-standard forms, which have also had an effect on the language. She does not feel that foreign teachers will be unreservedly welcomed or have an appreciable effect on the English as it is spoken by most students and teachers in Singapore, in contrast to Hong Kong, which has an officially sanctioned Native English-speaking teacher (NET) scheme. There is a feeling among Singaporeans that the local variety of English is a badge of national identity.

As for the lower status accorded to NNS teachers of English, Maria says that it is not widespread among the main employers of English teachers in Singapore, such as the Ministry of Education, universities, and polytechnics. Overall, she thinks that employers should consider the aims of the courses for which they hire teachers and spell out the skills and experience required instead of specifying skin colour, ethnicity, or country of origin.

Chapter 6

An English Teacher from the Expanding Circle

China, with a population of 1.3 billion, is the most populous country in the world. The Republic of China was formed in 1911, ending a lengthy period of feudalism. The People's Republic of China was established in 1949. After a period of enforced isolation, China has followed an "open door" policy for the past 30 years. Joining the World Trade Organization in 2001 and hosting the Olympic Games in 2008 are considered landmarks in China's development and modernization.

Although China is multi-ethnic, the Han nationality accounts for more than 90% of the population. The Chinese language consists of many dialects, Mandarin, Wu (spoken around the Shanghai area), and Cantonese (spoken in the southern region and in Hong Kong) being dominant. English language teaching in China has been through many changes since the early 1900s, usually following political upheavals. Due to their Communist ideologies, the Soviet Union and China were close allies from 1949, and Russian used to be the dominant foreign language taught in Chinese primary and secondary schools. As far as the teaching of foreign languages is concerned, perhaps the most significant event was the bitter ideological differences between China and the Soviet Union that arose in the 1960s. As a result, the teaching of Russian as a main foreign language declined and the teaching of English became popular again.[1]

The Story of Sihua

Our story begins in a village near Xuezhuang, a town in the Shandong Province. Born in 1970, Sihua (a pseudonym) grew up in a poor farmer's family with many children. In those days, despite their poverty, farmers in China preferred large families because the children could help with household work as well as on the farm.

Sihua's first school consisted of one building. She, her brothers, sisters, and other children walked to school. The school was poorly equipped and teachers only had chalk and blackboards; there wasn't even a radio at the school. Perhaps the only comfort was that students had textbooks for all their subjects. It was in this environment that Sihua, along with 50 or 60 classmates, studied subjects such as Chinese, math, nature, general knowledge, and history every day. All these subjects were taught by one teacher.

In those days, Sihua had no exposure to English at all; English was not taught in primary schools nor were there any English programs on radio. There were no newspapers or magazines in English, and Sihua's family did not own a TV.[2] Although there was no reading material in English, Sihua had access to Chinese language short novels and magazines such as *Novel Offprint*, *Liaoning Youth*, and *Novel Monthly*, which was first published in 1979. Access to these publications was possible only after the Cultural Revolution had ended. China was opening up to the world and most of the material in these novels and magazines contained items on this topic. She remembers listening on radio to popular Chinese music such as "North-West Wind" and "Story Time." The government's open economic policies not only encouraged economic development but also enriched reading materials.

Among all her teachers, Sihua remembers Zhong Zhaosi, her math teacher, and Nie Huaiju, her Chinese teacher; the latter was still teaching in the village school at the time of this interview. However, she believes that none of her teachers had received any systematic training in methodology or subject areas. They were only senior secondary school graduates employed by local communities. They became eligible for promotion and for employment by the state when they accumulated some years of teaching experience.

Junior Secondary Education

In 1983, at the age of 13, Sihua enrolled in Xuezhuang Central Middle School. At first, this middle school only had two classes, but gradually the number increased to six. There were more subjects than at the primary school. Chinese, English, math, physics, and chemistry were taught from the second year onwards, and biology and physiology from the third year. There were also more teachers. Sihua remembers a teacher named Zhang who taught her Chinese. He is now the Governor of Yi'nan County.

The teachers in the middle school may have been better trained than those in the primary school because their teaching methods were different. For example, during language lessons, primary school teachers asked students to copy new words ten times and memorize the texts. Those who failed to carry out these tasks were punished.[3] When asked to elaborate on the difference between her primary middle school teachers, Sihua replied:

> In general, teachers in the middle school were better trained and had better subject-matter knowledge. They were responsible, dedicated teachers. In contrast, teachers in the primary school did not have a serious attitude towards teaching and taught as if they were shepherds putting sheep out to the pasture. They did not treat their job or the students seriously. Often, they disappeared for the whole day after assigning us something to do.

Sihua remembers the names of her first and second English teachers. The English teachers were not as good as teachers of other subjects. According to Sihua, the teachers had studied English for two or three years in secondary school but had failed their college entrance examinations. So they returned home and became English teachers. They could speak only a little English and their English accent was "terrible."

At first, there were only two teachers for the English classes in the middle school. As the school grew, more and more teachers were hired. In general, the teachers taught English in Chinese because they were not capable of teaching in English except when reading the text, and then with very strong accents. The textbook was simply titled *English* but the front cover indicated that it was for use at junior secondary level. Other than the textbooks, Sihua recalls her teachers reading teachers' manuals and some other training materials. Sometimes they read English newspapers. They would teach pronunciation, grammar, and vocabulary. They required the students to do exercises such as constructing sentences, memorizing the usage of words, and reading and reciting texts. They also taught the students the International Phonetic Alphabet. In order to increase their English proficiency, students were advised to recite more.

Every textbook had about ten units. During the English lesson, a short text of about two pages was first read and explained by the teacher, in Chinese, point by point. Then the students recited the passages under the teacher's watchful eye, followed by further explanations by the teacher of the list of key words and expressions in the text. (Chinese translations of these words and expressions were included in the textbook.) For homework, students were asked to memorize the new vocabulary and expressions.[4] At the beginning of the next day's lesson, students would be questioned about what they had learned the previous day. With the encouragement of the teachers, most students not only memorized the vocabulary and expressions but also the entire textbook. According to Sihua, these endless memorizations may have been actually helpful to her in learning English because these words and expressions stuck in her mind.

The students had an English lesson every day so there were actually six teaching hours of English every week in addition to the self-studying periods in the morning and evening. Because the teachers didn't speak in English, the students rarely spoke English in class except when they answered questions. They didn't speak English at all after class. For extracurricular activities in terms of English studies, the students sometimes compiled various pieces of information into an English "newspaper" without much help from the teachers. They also read English newspapers and did the exercises in the papers. However, they rarely had opportunities to listen to English programs on the radio or watch any English on TV as there were limited channels available. When Sihua was at junior middle school, she found English really interesting because it was "a totally new language" to her. She learned well and the teacher liked her. She was "greatly attracted to English."

Senior Secondary Education

After graduating from the junior middle school, Sihua went to Fei Yang No.1 Senior Middle School, which had ten classes at the junior level and 18 classes at senior level. The school had nearly 2,000 students. Chinese, English, and math were the three most important subjects. In China, when students go to senior high school they choose either the arts or science streams. Sihua chose the arts stream so she studied politics, history and geography in addition to core courses such as Chinese, English, and math.

Sihua was impressed by her teachers at the senior middle school. They had received more systemic training than the junior middle school teachers. Most of them were university graduates. There were about 20 teachers of English in total, all locals. There were no foreign teachers; the school does not have foreign teachers even now. The teachers spoke some English in class, but not much; they still had strong accents but they spoke better English than her previous English teachers. Some teachers took undergraduate courses or did self-study. But the teaching methods were no different from those used by the junior middle school teachers; they taught English in Chinese and required the students to read, memorize, and recite.[5] They advised the students to be interested in the subject, encouraged them to cooperate with the teacher actively, and to be good at memorizing vocabulary, rules of grammar, and texts. So Sihua and her classmates did lots of exercises in preparation for examinations. It seemed as if students were learning English solely for the sake of passing exams, as is still the case today.

The English textbooks and teaching materials were compiled for nationwide use and published by People's Education Press. Again, the book was titled *English* but the front cover indicated that the book was for senior secondary students.[6] Grammar played an important role. There were six English classes each week, one class per day. Compared with the junior middle school, there were more students beginning to speak English in class. They had more contact with English and attached more importance to English. There were at least some extracurricular activities in terms of English studies; the students organized English clubs although not many activities were conducted. Occasionally, there were English speech contests. Other than the English textbooks, Sihua subscribed to and read some reference books and newspapers such as *English Coaching Paper* and *English Learning. English Coaching Paper* was published in Jilin Province and it had both a high school edition and a college edition. There were some English programs on TV but Sihua didn't have the time for TV. However, she did listen to some English teaching programs on the radio. Sihua didn't think English was difficult and was still very interested in English when she was at senior middle school. She had a sound foundation and continued to receive high marks in English. According to Sihua, "English was an important subject, and it was really important in the examinations."

Higher Education

After senior secondary school, Sihua entered Linyi Normal Specialized Postsecondary College, a teacher training institution. This institution is now known as the Linyi Teachers College and the English department alone has more than 2,000 students. The English curriculum included Intensive Reading, Extensive Reading, British Literature, American Literature, English Grammar, Listening Comprehension, Oral English, and Teaching Methodology.[7] The most important courses were Intensive Reading, Extensive Reading, Listening, and Oral English. For British and American Literature, some of the authors were Thomas Hardy, Charles Dickens, Jack London, Shakespeare, Ernest Hemingway, and Mark Twain.

The English department employed more than 20 teachers. Most of them had graduated from universities and some were at postgraduate level. A mixture of English and Chinese was used in class but more and more teachers tried to speak English, especially in oral English classes. Sihua was not taught by any foreign teachers but she had opportunities to interact with some who taught at other institutions and visited her college to conduct activities for students and give lectures.

Although her teachers still spoke with strong accents, their English was of a higher standard. They had a more systematic and flexible command of the English language. The students were asked "to learn everything by heart in the middle school. The 'four abilities' were quite popular at that time: the ability to read, write, recite, and apply." But the approach was quite different in college, according to Sihua. The teachers didn't insist on the students memorizing or reciting the material. In addition, the listening and oral English classes were closely related to daily life. The college teachers attached more importance to study skills and were more flexible in their teaching methods. Further, the teachers consciously communicated with the students in English. According to Sihua, she "didn't learn the same way as in the middle school. In college, students were required to develop more integrative abilities rather than accumulate knowledge only."

Sihua earned a diploma in English Education after two years at Linyi Normal Specialized Postsecondary College. As an English major, she had English classes every day on different subjects, about 30 classes per week, and there were more audiovisual materials and a special lab for listening and speaking. Some of the English materials were related to BBC programs. *Step by Step*, compiled by a professor at the Central China Normal University, was used as their listening textbook. It was considered a good book and had been used for many years. The audio-tapes had been recorded by native speakers.

When she was a sophomore, she found extensive reading quite difficult. Their textbook was *College English* compiled by Beijing Foreign Studies University. Especially in Book 3 and Book 4, the amount of new vocabulary increased sharply without a list of new words. She often spent the whole night looking up the words in the dictionary, which was boring and time-consuming. The other textbook was called *Advanced English*, which was full of excerpts from the classics. It was also difficult for students to fully comprehend some of the readings.

The students had access to some English TV programs and went to see English movies at the weekend. They conducted other extracurricular activities such as English parties, English sing-songs, and so on. They read a lot, too, especially in a special course called Extensive Reading, where they could read English classics. Sihua often listened to English radio programs on the BBC and the Voice of America (VOA). However, it was difficult for the students to fully understand what they heard on the radio.

Teaching Career

After graduation, Sihua was assigned to Zhangzhuang Central Middle School as a teacher of English by the local bureau of education. The school was not far from her village and most people were poor. On average, the annual income of a local family was only several hundred RMB. Because education was compulsory, all children were supposed to attend school but many quit after attending for a year or two.

English was a compulsory subject. Sihua first taught students who were around 12 or 13 years old, almost all of whom came from poor families. Despite their poverty, they had to pay tuition fees, the cost of textbooks, and incidental expenses. Since 2007, primary and secondary school students from rural areas do not have to pay school fees (He An E., personal communication). The textbooks alone cost about RMB100. For the English curriculum, People's Education Press had published a new textbook that was very communicative. The contents were about daily life and there was more emphasis on oral English, although the grammar component was not as systematic as before. The teachers had reference books, which provided detailed, step-by-step lesson plans and answer keys to exercises. The textbooks also provided homework exercises for students.

The textbook had been compiled through a joint effort between China and Britain and was the first of its kind. It was an attractive book with pictures. As required by the textbook and the curriculum, Sihua paid much attention to the students' listening and speaking. She taught in a mixture of English and Chinese for two reasons. Sometimes, she couldn't make herself understood by the students and at other times students had difficulty understanding what was taught because of their limited vocabulary. Her teaching method was mainly audiolingual as the textbook was compiled that way. For teaching aids, there were cassette recorders, tapes, and some wallcharts, as well as a small library, though it had only a few books and hardly any in English.

Sihua moved to the No.1 Middle School in 1996 after four years of teaching in the Zhangzhuang Central Middle School. She wanted a change in the work environment and in living conditions. Because of the expansion of the No. 1

Middle School, many new teaching positions had been created. Some teachers were transferred from other schools and new teachers were hired. Some teachers, including Sihua, also received promotions regularly from then on.

Sihua now teaches only senior middle school students as there are no junior middle school students at No.1 Middle School. Her students are between 16 and 18 years old. Many are from the countryside and are docile and diligent. Although the socioeconomic condition of her students is getting better now, 70% of them still live in poverty. Generally speaking, students from the towns are a little better off than those from the countryside and those from business families live in even better economic conditions.

At the No.1 Middle School, Sihua makes use of several sets of textbooks. The first book, *New Curriculum Criteria*, was jointly published by the People's Education Press and Longman Education Press. The textbook is closely related to daily life. Every unit is divided into four parts: listening, speaking, reading, and writing. Listening and speaking are in colloquial language while reading and writing are in relatively formal written language. There are pictures in the textbook. Sihua still uses the audiolingual method in her teaching. The students in this school concentrate on studies because of the keen competition for higher education opportunities. According to Sihua, "In the junior secondary school, students learned English because they were really interested in the language. They participated in the lessons actively and eagerly. But in the senior secondary school, students, especially the third-year ones, learn English under the pressure of university entrance exams." They are also shy and prefer to learn in their own manner. So the audiolingual is probably not the best method. In addition, reading and writing play a more important role. As a result, the classes are more teacher-centered.

According to Sihua, the teaching conditions are satisfactory. "After all, it is the No.1 Middle School."[8] There are more English books, newspapers, and magazines in the library, most of them related to pedagogy. They subscribe to *Foreign Language Teaching of Middle and Primary Schools*, a magazine, and two newspapers, *China Daily* and *21st Century*. Sihua reads a wide range of books. She wants to improve her level of teaching and also write something of her own. She has published a number of articles in Chinese language magazines for students.

People no longer listen to the radio because TV is so popular now. She logs on the Internet to search for information. The Internet is free of charge at school and she has access to some foreign sites. She usually watches news and some entertainment programs on TV. She does not watch TV serials as they are usually very long and she cannot afford the time every day. As there is no English environment, she seldom speaks English. There are no foreign teachers in No.1 Middle School but some foreigners are always invited to give lectures and organize some extracurricular activities, such as the English Corner.

Sihua has compiled many reading materials for the students. Some of them are adapted from the books used by university students, others from the Internet.

She can log on to some foreign websites, too, to find reading material for both primary students and middle school students.

Pre-service and In-service Training

During her training at the Linyi Normal Specialized Postsecondary College (the Teachers College), Sihua took some elective courses such as psychology and pedagogy in addition to the required courses for English teacher trainees. Although she didn't attend any other schools for further study, she has participated in many training courses, especially when the old textbooks were replaced by new ones. She attends training courses during summer and winter vacations to accumulate credit hours for future promotions. Organized by the Education Bureau, these courses are usually given by experts in various subjects.

Sihua took a three-year distance education course at Qufu Normal University in order to obtain a BA in English Education. During that time she studied at home, occasionally attending lectures at the University. The courses covered were similar to those in the Teachers College but at higher level and were more challenging. They included Extensive Reading, Intensive Reading, selected readings of English and American Literature, vocabulary, and linguistics. In literature, the readings were again from Thomas Hardy, Charles Dickens, Jack London, Shakespeare, Ernest Hemingway, Mark Twain, and some other authors. The course also included the Romantic poets. When she returned her assignments to her teachers, they only marked the important parts. The students did not wish to take challenging examinations and preferred "open book" tests.[9]

Sihua wants to improve her English proficiency. Some of her former classmates have obtained Master's (degrees) or even doctoral degrees and found more satisfactory jobs. She was on a par with them when they were classmates but now she has been left behind and wishes to catch up.

Attitudes and Perceptions

Sihua says that, as a teacher, she is not as well off as those who work in banks and telecommunication companies because they have better incomes. Now, many people have private cars and live in splendid houses. Work, study, and family are equally important to Sihua, so she divides her time accordingly. During the day, she goes to work while her child goes to school. She does housework after work and spends some time on research and self-study in the evenings. If there is something urgent in the family, she will deal with it as soon as possible. But her work and study are very important to her.

Sihua thinks that to be an English teacher in China has both advantages and disadvantages. As a teacher, she is in the forefront of acquiring new knowledge and leads a relatively predictable life. On the downside, the income is not satisfactory. As English language study in China becomes more and more important, the status of teachers of English should improve as well. In fact, English teachers are already better off than teachers of other subjects.

When asked what she thinks of English teaching in China, she says that she has thought much about English teaching and also written some articles on it. The curriculum is too bound to the college entrance examination. According to Sihua,

> If you ask me the difference between the education now and that of ten years ago, I am sorry to say that not much has changed. We still teach to the examinations. Often the students are forced to study something just because it might appear in the exam papers.

Sihua thinks it is difficult to change the situation because the college entrance examination cannot be done away with. Any reform of the educational system must happen gradually. If there were no college entrance examinations, teachers would be freer to motivate students to study and to enhance their abilities to listen and speak. Some teachers have the desire and the ability to do this but are reluctant because the students won't be able to get high marks in the examinations. Because they are evaluated by the ratio of successful university candidates, teachers are under pressure to perform, since their bonus and credit all depend on this single criterion.

Sihua thinks that the new National English Curriculum for Chinese schools is a synthesis of the standards of many countries and is idealistic and impractical. The curriculum is difficult to implement. For example, one area of confusion is the credit system,[10] but the teachers have no idea who has the final right to speak on the system. Is it the school itself or the administration at a higher level? In reality, the curriculum reform will not work so long as the college entrance examination remains the decisive factor.

With regard to English being a compulsory subject from Grade 3 of primary school, Sihua's view is that the implementation of the policy should be based on theory and research. In many countries, English is taught from the early years of primary school. Although educational systems around the world have not agreed on the age at which foreign languages should be first taught, it is generally accepted that the earlier, the better. Although the Chinese government invests much money and energy in English education now, Sihua wonders how many jobs in the future will require a knowledge of English. She has read similar comments on the topic on the Internet, that the output may not justify the input.

Sihua's school does not employ any native speaker English teachers. Even at college, she was not taught by foreign teachers; invited foreign teachers gave only occasional lectures. After she graduated, she attended a two-month training course that was taught by several foreigners who were native speakers of English. The foreign teachers taught very differently from the Chinese teachers.

In general, Chinese teachers taught methodically, sticking to the textbooks, while foreign teachers often seemed to teach randomly, as if they had never prepared for the lessons. But students do learn something practical from the foreign teachers. According to Sihua, this is the difference between Chinese teachers and foreign teachers. From foreign teachers, they learn some practical skills that help them in the classroom. She thinks that the Chinese pay too much attention to academic knowledge and systematic learning.

As a Chinese teacher, Sihua feels somewhat inferior to foreign teachers when she speaks to them. She knows a few Canadian and Australian teachers and feels that sometimes it is difficult to make herself understood. Although she finds it easy to talk about topics related to daily life, it really bothers her when it comes to professional topics because much jargon is involved in such conversations. She thinks it would be good if foreign teachers can teach listening and speaking in No.1 Middle School, so students can practice English with them.

Chapter 7

From Worlds Apart: The Lives of Two English Teachers

I allowed the two previous chapters to stand alone without discussion or analysis for a clear reason. I wanted the voices of the two English teachers to be heard with the least intrusion. Hence, part of this chapter will be devoted to a discussion and analysis of the issues and concerns that arise for ELT from the narratives of the two teachers.

Why are the life stories of these English teachers important? For one, as pointed out earlier, we do not have much information on NNS English teachers, especially those living and teaching in Outer and Expanding Circles. As a result, every life story adds depth to the research base on English language teaching. Secondly, the publication of these narratives empowers these often marginalized teachers by giving them a "voice" and encouraging them to view events from their own perspectives.

Nevertheless, a question arises. How reliable are these accounts? By formulating the interview questions, I have no doubt determined the contents of the narratives to some extent. Nevertheless, the two teachers are from social, economic, cultural, educational, linguistic, and geographical contexts that I have been familiar with for most of my life. These teachers are not from Africa, Europe, or South America. Instead, they are from Asia. My upbringing and education in Sri Lanka, my 14 years of living and teaching in Hong Kong, and my frequent and extended travels within Asia have provided me with a substantial knowledge of the region and their ethnic, socioeconomic, and educational backgrounds. Hence, the interview questions I formulated were bound to elicit the most relevant information on the two teachers.

Another issue is the trustworthiness of these stories, their validity and reliability to use the jargon of research. As Hayes (2005), who explored the lives of three Sri Lankan English teachers pointed out, trustworthiness can be measured against verifiable facts and the internal consistency of the narratives. The life stories can also be triangulated with government reports and classroom observations.

English teachers have been classified as NS and NNS, as teaching in ESL or EFL contexts, as being from the Inner, Outer, and Expanding Circles. In the literature relating to English language teaching, teachers from ESL contexts and those from the Inner Circle have received more international exposure because most publications relating to ELT originate in these contexts and also because an overwhelming degree of research relating to ELT also occurs in these contexts. But the bulk of English language teaching now occurs in the Expanding Circle in countries such as China. The dearth of knowledge about these teachers in the Expanding Circle is strongly felt by teacher-scholars such as myself who have taught and researched ELT at both ESL and EFL contexts, in Inner, Outer, and Expanding Circle countries. Hence, the chapter on the English teacher in China should fill a void.

As I have stated elsewhere in the book (see Chapter 8, for instance), I am disappointed with the lack of commitment to the English language by many NNS colleagues. Despite being teachers of English and therefore role models to their students, their use of English is often limited to the classroom. Hence, the comparison of two English teachers, an older teacher with a lifelong commitment to English and a younger teacher, from the Expanding Circle, who represented the new generation of English teachers. For the former, I chose a teacher from Malaysia, a former British colony, whose background was similar to mine in Sri Lanka, another former colony of Britain. I could relate directly to her socioeconomic background, her development as an English teacher, and her day-to-day interactions with the English language.

Why did I choose a teacher from China to represent the Expanding Circle? In terms of English language teaching, the statistics on China are staggering. In Chapter 2, based on official statistics, I estimated that the number of English learners in Chinese public schools and universities to be around 230 million. When learners at private language centers and those obtaining tuition individually are added to this number, the total number of English learners in China could be as high as 600 million (see Niu & Wolff, 2004). To take a specific example, "College English" refers to the English language instruction in both four-year universities and three-year colleges for non-English majors. Students majoring in arts, sciences, engineering, management, law, and medical science constitute students of "College English." In 2006, about 5.4 million students were enrolled on such courses at 1,867 universities and colleges in China (see http://www.edu.cn/jiao_yu_fa_zhan_498/20080901/t20080901_321919.shtml).

What about English teachers who teach the vast numbers of students at primary and secondary levels as well? There is no doubt that an army of English teachers has to be employed. Once again, accurate numbers are not available. According to Bolton (2004), an expert in World Englishes and a scholar familiar with the ELT situation in China, the number of secondary level English teachers in China was around 500,000. Liao (2004) estimates the number of English teachers at the primary level in China to be 1.5 million. Despite these staggering numbers, only a few personal narratives of English teachers have been published. Two of the most prominent, by Liu (2001) and He (2005), are by Chinese teacher-scholars who have obtained doctoral degrees from foreign universities and now teach in the USA and Hong Kong respectively. To my knowledge, no personal account of an English teacher at primary or secondary level has been published in English; hence my selection of a Chinese teacher at the secondary level to represent the Expanding Circle. Ideally, the comparison should have been between two teachers from China, one from an older generation and the other a relative novice. However, due to the Cultural Revolution, the recent history of ELT in China does not extend beyond 30 years, and older teachers with a lengthy commitment to English no longer appear to serve at the primary or secondary level.

The interview with the teacher from Malaysia, now resident in Singapore, was conducted mainly by e-mail with one face-to-face meeting. The chapter is mainly a paraphrase of her responses. The interview with the teacher from China was conducted in Chinese by a professor of English, then transcribed, and revised a number of times in consultation with the professor who conducted the interview. The final version was also checked by a number of scholars familiar with ELT in China. In writing style, the two chapters are distinctly different because I have attempted to maintain the voice of the two teachers.

Socioeconomic Backgrounds and Early Education

Although born two decades apart and in countries widely separated linguistically, culturally, and geographically, Maria and Sihua share one characteristic: they were both born to economically impoverished families. However, beyond the fact that both chose to be English teachers, Maria and Sihua have little in common in their family backgrounds and upbringing.

Maria was born with a distinct advantage for a future English teacher. Malaya was a British colony at the time of her birth and English was the medium of instruction in government schools which Maria began to attend from the age of six. As the only child of parents who spoke separate Chinese dialects, Maria grew up in a multilingual neighborhood that would encourage a young child to "pick up" languages easily. In contrast, Sihua was born to a large farming family in rural China. Her family and neighborhood were monolingual. Being the final years of the Cultural Revolution, English was not taught at the primary school where Sihua began her schooling. She was first taught English at junior secondary school at the age of 13, thereby missing the critical stage for optimum language acquisition.

The English environment that Maria first encountered was rich in substance and variety. English was not limited to the classroom; Maria heard prayers recited and hymns being sung in English and was taught to sing (in English) and move to music. She joined a catechism class where prayers and church precepts were taught. According to Maria, her teachers—Catholic nuns from Ireland, France, and Malaya—spoke "perfect" English. In contrast, Sihua's

English teachers spoke with a "terrible" accent, had only become English teachers because they failed the college entrance examination, and taught English in Chinese. During English lessons, the textbook was explained by the teachers in Chinese, point by point. Homework meant memorizing new words and expressions which led some students to memorize the entire textbook. Although Sihua compiled an English "newspaper," she rarely listened to English programs on radio or watched them on TV because such programs were not available. In contrast, Maria read anything she could lay her hands on and "devoured" Enid Blyton books, popular among children in Britain and the colonies.

Maria continued her junior and secondary education at the same convent school. The medium of instruction was English, thus reinforcing English throughout the curriculum. The English textbooks were supplemented with readings from the classics, initially in simplified form. Students were not allowed to use their first languages in school and thus had to communicate in English. Maria spoke English with friends outside school as well. In secondary school, her leisure reading included both fiction and nonfiction works. For Sihua, on the other hand, the medium of instruction continued to be Chinese in senior secondary school as well. Although the number of English teachers at her school had increased to around 20, and many of them were university graduates, they did not converse in English. They did speak some English in class but still spoke with strong accents. The teaching methods remained the same, the pattern being read, memorize, and recite. Grammar continued to play an important role. For extracurricular reading, Sihua read a few "newspapers" meant for students.

Higher Education

The disparity noted between Maria and Sihua begins to widen when they leave secondary school to enter university and teachers' college respectively. Maria entered the University of Malaya, the most prestigious tertiary institution in Malaysia and highly respected for its academic standards in the region as well. The curriculum was modeled on British universities. The teachers were both local and expatriate. Maria majored in English literature; Shakespeare, Chaucer, and Eliot were a must. Continuing her love of books, she took the opportunity to read widely beyond the curriculum and also participated in plays, poetry readings, and in the Literary and Drama societies while also writing for the campus newspaper. She only spoke English.

On completing secondary school, Sihua entered a teachers' college. Although the curriculum included coursework in British and American literature, the emphasis was on intensive and extensive reading, listening, and oral English, generally considered "skills" courses. Memorizing and reciting was less emphasized and the English course contents related more to daily life. Teachers, all of whom were locals, communicated with students in English and there was a conscious effort to develop language ability instead of accumulating knowledge. However, vocabulary learning was a tedious task, whole nights spent on looking up words in the dictionary. Extensive reading, too, was part of coursework, not necessarily undertaken for pleasure. During this period, Sihua began to watch English movies, TV programs, and also began to listen to BBC and VOA (Voice of America) broadcasts. She later obtained a distance degree in English Education, studying from home. Once again, the emphasis was on courses such as intensive and extensive reading and vocabulary, although courses in British and American literature were also included.

Teaching and Professional Growth

Straight from university, without any teacher training, Maria was appointed as an English teacher to a Catholic boys' school in her hometown. She taught English language and literature. Students in her classes wrote summaries, responses to comprehension questions based on readings, and compositions. The medium of instruction was English. In keeping with prevailing practices, the classes were teacher-centered. After only a year at the school, Maria was transferred to a local teachers' college to teach courses in English language, teaching methodology, and linguistics. Her students came from all over Malaysia.

Sihua, too, was assigned to a local school upon graduation from teachers' college, but her students were from rural, poverty-stricken families. She liked the attractive textbook, the emphasis on oral English, and the helpful reference books. Sihua taught in both English and Chinese, using mainly the audiolingual method. After four years, she moved to a prestigious senior middle school where she continues to teach mainly rural students with a sprinkling of relatively affluent students from town. The students are diligent because they have to compete fiercely for limited university places. Both Sihua and her students have access to more English books, newspapers, and magazines.

Attitudes and Perceptions

One reason that Maria became a teacher is the prevailing view in the 1960s that teaching was a suitable job for women. Maria is now confident in her pedagogical skills while becoming more reflective on teaching, the state of English in Malaysia and Singapore (where she teaches now), and on the role of English in her family. After four decades on the job, she still spends 10 hours or more in the office and takes student papers home for grading. Reflecting on her years at the teachers' college, Maria recalls the declining English proficiency of the teacher trainees and attributes it to the downgrading of English in Malaysia in the interest of nationalism. Even in the case of English trainees, her dilemma was whether to enhance their English proficiency or to teach linguistics and teaching methodology in the limited time available. Having lived and taught in Malaysia and Singapore, Maria is in a position to compare how English has fared in these countries. While Malaysia neglected English, Singapore continued with English as the medium of instruction. As a result, Singapore has enough qualified teachers who can teach English confidently.

Sihua was greatly attracted to the English language when she first encountered it at junior middle school. Despite having to plough through the dictionary in order to enhance her vocabulary, she sustained her interest in English through secondary school and teachers' college. She is satisfied with her current teaching conditions though not with her salary as an English teacher. She envies her classmates who have gone to better-paying jobs in other fields. She thinks that the English curriculum is bound too strongly to public examinations. Sihua is able to analyze the advantages and disadvantages of being an English teacher in a China that has been transformed to a market-oriented society.

Discussion and Analysis of the Narratives

My reasons for titling this chapter "From worlds apart" should be clear to the reader now. Maria was exposed to English early in her life while Sihua had to wait until middle school. Maria studied in environments rich in English and was taught by local and expatriate teachers who were fluent users of English. Sihua, when she eventually began learning English, was left in the hands of teachers who themselves were barely fluent in English, taught in Chinese, and encouraged to memorize and recite at the expense of communication. Her environment, lacking in English speakers, English books, magazines, newspapers, regular English programs on radio or TV, did not promote the acquisition of English at all.

Sihua did not choose her environment. Since the establishment of the People's Republic in 1949, ELT in China has seen cataclysmic changes, rising in favor at times and then being banished from the curriculum a few years later. The Cultural Revolution, which lasted from the mid-1960s to the mid-1970s, is widely acknowledged as a time of social and economic upheaval, much to the detriment of ELT in China. Most schools and universities were shut down and English was considered a weapon for political struggle. Sihua was born while the Cultural Revolution raged and English was barely making a comeback when she began schooling.

However, a question arises: how representative are these narratives of English teachers from the Outer and Expanding Circles? Alas, I only wish Maria's narrative was typical. When I was a teacher trainee in Sri Lanka in the early 1970s, in my cohort of 150 classmates, at least half would have been similar to Maria in terms of their fluency in and use of English. They came from English medium schools, many from English-speaking homes, and they were at ease with the language. They read English newspapers and magazines, listened to English pop songs on the radio (Sri Lanka did not have TV at that time), and conversed with each other freely in English. Forty years on in Sri Lanka, among the younger English teachers who have come from backgrounds with little English in their day-to-day lives, having studied English as another subject in non-English medium schools, English proficiency is at an appallingly low level. For many of these teachers, teaching English is another job like teaching physics or mathematics and their use of the language ends when they leave school at the end of the day. They would rather watch TV programs, read newspapers and magazines, and converse in their first languages, Sinhala or Tamil. Proficient users of English obtain more lucrative employment in the mercantile sector, shunning the low-paying teaching positions. The situation has deteriorated to such an extent that the government has begun to conduct "spoken English" classes for English teachers in public schools. Even in affluent Hong Kong, as I note in Chapter 8, the typical English teacher is not a fluent user of the language. This phenomenon, where recent generations of English teachers from Outer Circle countries such as Hong Kong, Malaysia, and Sri Lanka, for example, have shown a steady decline in their English proficiency, is alarming because the situation in Expanding Circle countries is even worse. Sihua's story is only too typical. Multiplied a million-fold, it does not indicate a positive outlook in areas where ELT is growing the most.

As He (2005) points out, the open door policy that began in the 1970s in China has had a major impact on ELT because English has risen in importance for internal use as well as for dealing with other countries. No longer limited to the school curriculum, English has now become part of the workplace and of daily communication. Nevertheless, the linguistic environment in China described by Sihua is illustrative of the situation in many Expanding Circle countries where English is being taught. In Japan and Korea, countries that are more affluent than China, the governments have implemented schemes where NS English teachers are recruited to teach in schools because local English teachers are deemed incompetent. For instance, the Japan Exchange and Teaching (JET) program recruits native speakers to serve as assistant language teachers in Japanese schools. This government-run program has an annual budget of approximately US$500 million (Benoit, 2003).

After more than four decades as an English teacher in Asia and North America, I am not optimistic about the English fluency of new English teachers. For many, despite the English language providing their livelihood, English only plays a minor role in their lives, more instrumental than integrative. Despite the concept of World Englishes gaining wide acceptance, many of these teachers see English as an alien tongue. Because the *status quo* has now become acceptable, there is little incentive for these teachers to change. Even among my NNS university teacher colleagues in English and linguistics, few see the need for leisure reading or much interest in politics or economics. Conversations with them do not extend beyond topics relating to our shared disciplines because they have little interest or knowledge of other matters. Indeed, Maria, whose reading and interests are wide-ranging, belongs to a species in the Outer Circle that is rapidly becoming extinct!

More Research on NNS English Teachers

In Chapters 3 and 4, I summarized and discussed the self-perceptions of NNS English teachers as well as how they were perceived by their students. In the rest of this chapter, studies that did not belong in the previous chapters will be summarized and discussed. Although the studies on perceptions are vital to the growth of a new area of research into a somewhat controversial domain, the studies included below are equally important because they go beyond perceptions and also contribute to a growing body of research.

Three studies conducted in Hong Kong are noteworthy here. In the first two, Forde (1996) and Luk (1998) both examined Hong Kong students' attitudes towards NS and NNS accents. Forde's subjects were 72 Chinese-speaking elementary school students who were asked to rate five tape-recorded accents according to five criteria. The accents were Standard American English, Australian English, Hong Kong English, RP English, and Yorkshire English. The criteria included friendliness, comprehensibility, level of education, ability in English, and ability in teaching. In order to obtain a more objective view of the comprehensibility of the accents, the students also responded to some listening comprehension questions. The Hong Kong accent was rated the least educated, least proficient in English, and the least effective for an English teacher. However, the responses to listening comprehension questions indicated that the students understood the Hong Kong speaker well. Forde concludes that "language learners in Hong Kong need to be taught to have a more positive attitude to their own variety" of English (p. 70).

Luk (1998) hypothesized that Hong Kong learners of English would be aware of a distinct Hong Kong accent and that they would display more empathy for the Hong Kong accent than for British RP. Luk's subjects were 66 secondary school students in Hong Kong, all Cantonese speakers. They responded to two questionnaires, the first after listening to tape recordings of a Hong Kong English accent and a British accent. In the second questionnaire, the students listened to three English sentences read by eight speakers, four of whom were NS of English and four of whom were Hong Kong speakers. The students had to agree or disagree with the following statement: "I think that most Hong Kong people speak English like him/her." The students' responses to the first questionnaire are more relevant to our purpose.

Nearly 100% of the subjects correctly identified the Hong Kong accent. A comparison of their reactions to the two accents, measured by three statements ("like the English he speaks," "like my English teacher(s) to speak like him," "want to speak English the way he speaks"), indicated that nearly 90% of the subjects preferred the NS accent, 86% wanted their English teachers to speak like the NS, and nearly 94% wished to speak like the NS. Discussing her research, Luk observes that the NNS accent had become an object of ridicule and that some of her subjects laughed upon hearing it.

In another study conducted in 2001, Luk aimed to determine the views and feelings of secondary school students in Hong Kong about the Native English-Speaker Teacher (NET) scheme in operation in local schools. Under the NET scheme, which was first introduced in 1987 and expanded in 1995, NS English teachers are hired from Inner Circle countries to teach English in local primary and secondary schools. Luk administered a survey to 212 second-ary students who were encouraged to write their responses freely in their first language. Overall, the students had a positive reaction towards being taught by NETs and to having more NETs in their schools. Analyzing these results, Luk states that local NNS English teachers face a daunting task in gaining the confidence of their students and suggests that these teachers extend "their English repertoire for social and personal interaction" (p. 34), capitalize on NS resources, and establish themselves as multi-competent English professionals.

McNeill (2005) notes that teachers who are more aware of the language difficulties of their students are more effective because they can pay attention to learners' actual needs. Conversely, teachers who are less aware of their students' difficulties may neglect areas where the students need the teachers' help. Based on these assumptions, McNeill investigated NS and NNS English teachers in Hong Kong, asking his subjects to identify the sources of difficulty in a reading passage. In addition to the 65 English teachers, 200 Cantonese-speaking secondary school students also participated in the study. The teachers were classified as "experts" and "novices." Experts were experienced, trained graduate teachers and novices were those still attending initial teacher training. All the NNS teachers used Cantonese as their dominant language but none of the NS teachers had studied Cantonese formally.

The students were given a 600-word reading passage and tested on their understanding of the vocabulary in the passage. The teachers were requested to make predictions on the difficulties that the students would encounter in the passage. Data analysis showed that the NS teachers failed to predict the words that the students found difficult. In contrast, the NNS teachers were more accurate in their predictions. In fact, both expert and novice NNS teachers' predictions correlated significantly with the students' difficulties. McNeill concludes that teachers who share their students' L1 "have a distinct advantage in knowing where their students' language difficulties lie" (p. 116).

Claiming a need for research on the language awareness of "Good language teachers," Andrews & McNeill (2005) investigated three highly experienced graduate NNS English teachers, two teaching in Hong Kong and one in Britain. (A "good" language teacher was defined as one who had obtained a distinction in the practicum section of professional training.) The data came from results of a test on language awareness, observations of lessons, interviews, and stimulated recall based on video recordings of teaching.

In the grammar component of the language awareness test, the three subjects did not fare much better than a group of 187 teachers who had taken the test previously. The latter group of teachers lacked professional training and most had only a few years of English teaching experience. Andrews & McNeill note that, in the vocabulary component of the language awareness test, two of the subjects could not explain the basis for their vocabulary error correction. In their pedagogical practices based on observations of lessons and interviews, the subjects displayed a well developed sense of teacher language awareness. Nevertheless, they revealed certain limitations; in the case of one teacher, of subject matter as well as the possibility for students to misunderstand her input. In the case of the second teacher from Hong Kong, her treatment of vocabulary could cause misunderstanding among the students. In fact, during the follow-up interviews, one of the teachers admitted that she was "not very good at vocabulary" (p. 170). As for characteristics of teacher language awareness, Andrews & McNeill observe that all three teachers showed a willingness to engage with language, that is the content of learning. To their credit, content issues formed the basis of their "thinking, planning, and teaching" (p. 170). Further, all three teachers were aware of their own limitations with regard to subject matter knowledge and reflection on the content of learning had become part of their teaching behavior. In conclusion, Andrews & McNeill claim that even "good language teachers" need to enhance their teacher language awareness.

NNS students, many coming from abroad, form a significant presence in MA TESOL programs in the United States. As a component of their professional training, the practicum, these teacher trainees are paired to teach with local ESL teachers. Some of these "host" teachers have resisted the presence of NNS teacher trainees in their classes citing complaints about the trainees' low English proficiency, unfamiliarity with American culture, and their students' preference for NS teachers. In this context, Nemtchinova (2005) conducted a study focusing on host teachers' evaluations of the NNS teacher trainees. The participants were 56 host teachers from middle and high schools, community colleges, and universities. Their trainees were from Argentina, Brazil, Chile, Japan, Korea, Pakistan, Poland, Russia, Slovakia, South Africa, Taiwan, and Turkey. About 88% of the trainees were novice teachers with no previous teaching experience. The evaluation criteria used by the host teachers were the trainees' personal qualities, command of English, teaching organization, lesson implementation, awareness of American culture, feedback provided to students, and the trainees' self-evaluations. For our purpose in this volume, the critical criteria are command of English and awareness of American culture.

Command of the language was correctness of structure and vocabulary, general intelligibility (adequacy of pronunciation and intonation patterns), fluency, authenticity, adjustment to students' level of language, appropriateness of the use of linguistics terms, and presenting a good model of English in all communication situations. On correctness of structure and general intelligibility, nearly 80% of the host teachers ranked their trainees as good and excellent. For fluency authenticity, adjustment, and linguistic terminology, too, similarly high ratings were given. In some comments, such as "correct but somewhat limited in variety" and "correct but not colloquial," the host teachers did point out shortcomings they observed in individual trainees. With regard to cultural awareness, the host teachers again ranked the trainees highly in familiarity with American culture and showed an "acute awareness of the difficulties involved in adapting to American culture" in line with the needs of their ESL students from abroad.

Nemtchinova points out that the host teachers commented positively on the NNS teacher trainees' knowledge of grammar, empathy with ESL students, the ability to share language learning experiences and cultural backgrounds, and to serve as role models. A number of host teachers commented on the trainees' need to improve their pronunciation and English in general. However, host teachers' comments did not indicate that cultural differences had affected the trainees' teaching. Keeping in mind that most of the trainees were inexperienced teachers, the shortcomings noted by the host teachers could be typical of such trainees regardless of language background.

In a wide-ranging study, Moussu (2006) surveyed students, teachers, and administrators of Intensive English Programs (IEP) in the United States. The student and teacher surveys have already been summarized in Chapters 3 and 4. Of the five research questions, the last was directed at administrators of Intensive English Programs (IEP), querying them for their opinions of teachers. Specifically, the research questions sought to compare the opinions of the program administrators on their teachers with the attitudes of students in these IEPs.

Twenty-one program administrators responded to the questionnaire and, on the whole, their views correlated with those of students regarding their teachers. NNS teachers' pedagogical skills ("curricular flexibility," "creativity in the classroom"), high standards ("dedication"), and expectations on student performance were seen as strengths. NNS teachers were also praised as good role models and for being able to understand the difficulties faced by their (ESL) students. In fact, all the administrators agreed or strongly agreed that NNS teachers were as effective as their NS counterparts in the classroom. However, foreign accents, an over-emphasis on grammar, and low self-esteem (which hindered their teaching) were seen as weaknesses.

Conclusion

In view of the considerable number of studies conducted on NNS English teachers' self-perceptions and their students' perceptions of the teachers, the studies summarized in this chapter appear to be insufficient both in terms of range and number. More life stories of English teachers, such as those from

Malaysia and China, will not only enrich our research but will also provide the data to predict the future of ELT and textbook design, and plan teacher-training curricula. For instance, the need for language skills courses in teacher-training programs is apparent from Sihua's narrative as well as in Nemtchinova's (2005) study. Another contribution made by Nemtchinova's study is the clearance of misconceptions on host teachers' views of NNS teacher trainees.

The implications of the three studies conducted in Hong Kong (Forde, 1996; and Luk, 1998, 2001) could be discouraging for NNS English teachers in Hong Kong. Local Cantonese-speaking students appear to have no respect for Hong Kong English accents and, by extension, local NNS English teachers. However, Cheung's (2002) study conducted among university students in Hong Kong suggests that the students begin to respect local English teachers as they gain more exposure to NNS as well as NS teachers. McNeill's (2005) study also makes a distinct contribution in raising the profile of local English teachers, especially in Hong Kong, because it indicates that teachers who share a common language with their students are more effective since they are able to pay more attention to learners' language difficulties. Andrews & McNeill (2005), on the other hand, imply that labeling language teachers as "good" does not imply "finished products"; such teachers may still need language enhancement to be effective in the classroom.

Chapter 8

Extrinsic and Intrinsic Challenges Faced by NNS English Teachers

Although NNS in the United States could be proud of what they have achieved in recent years, the discriminatory attitude towards NNS English teachers—from employers, students, NS colleagues, and parents of students—does not appear to have changed much in the rest of the world. Based on my observations in Asia, where I have lived and taught English for more than 25 years, NNS teachers there face the highest levels of discrimination. This is a result of more and more NS being attracted to English teaching jobs in Asia as a result of the regions' rising prosperity.

Extrinsic Challenges Faced by NNS Teachers

Even in the United States, discrimination appears to exist in hiring practices. In Chapter 2 I referred to the study by Mahboob, Uhrig, Newman, & Hartford (2004), which showed that NNS teachers are still a minority in college-level intensive English language programs in the USA. Of the 1,425 teachers employed in the 118 intensive English programs they surveyed, only 112 (7.9%) were NNS and most of them had been hired as part-timers. According to the majority of program administrators, native speaker status was an important criterion in the hiring of English teachers in these intensive programs. Noting that this low figure is disproportionate to the high number of NNS graduate students enrolled in MA TESOL and similar teacher-education programs in the US, the researchers attribute the low figure to the preference given by most (59.8%) program administrators to "native English speakers" in hiring practices.

In the United Kingdom, Clark & Paran (2007) conducted a similar study published under the explicit title "The employability of non-native teachers of EFL," focusing on hiring practices in the UK. They surveyed administrators responsible for hiring English teachers at British Council-accredited private language schools, universities and higher education institutions, and further education institutions. When making hiring decisions, 72.3% of the 90 respondents judged the "native English speaker criterion" to be either moderately or very important. The results of Clark & Paran (2007) strongly support Mahboob et al.'s (2004) conclusions that NNS teachers are, in effect, "children of a lesser English." Despite more than a decade of advocacy, prejudices against the hiring of NNS English teachers continue to exist in the main English-speaking countries.

In Asia, a number of reasons could be attributed for the discrimination faced by NNS English teachers. First, the "native speaker fallacy" that Phillipson (1992) first identified still prevails in most of Asia. In many Asian countries, NS teachers are still considered to be more competent in English and the variety of English they speak (usually a British dialect) is considered to be superior to the variety spoken by indigenous English teachers. This is partly because local English teachers are themselves not competent users of the English language. In a strange extension of the "native speaker fallacy," any Caucasian speaker of English (even Eastern Europeans who speak it as a second or foreign language) are automatically considered to be native speakers of English. To cite one example, Ozgur Parlak, who is from Turkey and is Caucasian, says that he was selected for an English-teaching position in Thailand more on his looks than his qualifications. He was referred to as "farang" (a term used for white westerners) instead of "khak kaao," a term used for white middle-easterners (personal communication).

Another reason for the prevalence of the fallacy is the indigenous English teachers' unawareness of the rise in the NNS movement and the respect that NNS English teachers have earned in ESL contexts. Academic journals, the Internet, listservs, and other sources for dissemination of information that are taken for granted in more affluent countries are simply not available or accessible to English teachers who live and work in some resource-poor Asian countries. These teachers are simply unaware of current trends in our profession. I recall a conversation with one such teacher in an Asian country. She would not believe that NNS English teachers were actually teaching English to NS students in the United States.

The result is that Asia is awash with Caucasians (not all of them NS of English) who are able to obtain English teaching jobs at their whim and fancy. Although some arrive with valid qualifications and experience in TESOL, many do not. These traveling teachers pose a major challenge to qualified indigenous teachers in terms of employment. The mushrooming of private "English Schools" or "academies" has been a common phenomenon in Asia. They are run by businessmen who are aware of the attraction of Caucasian NS teachers of English, if not for students, for their parents, who pay the tuition. Although indigenous NNS teachers may not care to teach at these "schools," the schools do help to propagate the native speaker fallacy and affect these NNS employment prospects in more formal institutions. I will refer to this in the Hong Kong context later in this chapter.

What attracts these traveling NS teachers to Asia? In Chapter 2 I listed the annual per capita incomes of a number of Asian countries and indicated that countries with higher per capita incomes with the ability to pay better salaries to expatriate English teachers attracted most NS teachers. In fact, they offer salaries on par with those in the West, with the added attraction of often not requiring teaching or professional qualifications. Accordingly, Japan, Hong Kong, Taiwan, and Korea are popular destinations, while few of these teachers would travel to Bangladesh, India, or Indonesia in search of employment. The private English Schools in countries with low per capita incomes are unable to offer salaries attractive enough for NS teachers.

In Chapter 2 I also referred to a popular website (www.transitionsabroad.com) in order to show the ease with which often unqualified NS obtain English teaching positions in Asia. Another site, which is specific to Thailand, is www.ajarn.com, which lists English teaching positions in that country. Although Thailand only has an annual per capita income of US$2,720, it is considered a haven for expatriate travelers who revel in its cuisine and easy-going, inexpensive lifestyle.

In previous chapters I also referred to the Native English Teacher (NET) scheme in Hong Kong, which employs qualified NS English teachers in primary and secondary schools, and the Japan Exchange and Teaching (JET) program, which employs mainly young, unqualified NS graduates to carry out team teaching with Japanese teachers of English. Korea, too, has a NS program, the English Program in Korea (EPIK), established in 1995, which follows the JET model and recruits English NS to enhance the English-speaking abilities of Korean students and teachers.

In Hong Kong, the NET scheme has been criticized for being "linguistic imperialism in the story of English in Hong Kong" (Boyle, 1997) and as neocolonization disguised as a language improvement measure (Lai, 1999). A local English teacher, Lung (1999), claims that the special treatment given to NET teachers—who are paid twice as much as local teachers in addition to being given housing and travel allowances—marginalizes, demoralizes, and diminishes the usefulness of local NNS English teachers.

Another extrinsic challenge faced by NNS English teachers across the world comes in the form of keynote speakers at local language conferences. Keynote speakers, who are usually experts in their respective areas within applied linguistics, are the star attractions at any conference and are often admired as role models whose theories and viewpoints are considered authoritative. Often, for conferences conducted in EFL contexts dominated by NNS English teachers, the keynote speakers tend to be NS from ESL contexts. This phenomenon not only perpetuates the native speaker fallacy, but also is ironic because the theories and pedagogics expounded by these "traveling keynote speakers" are irrelevant in EFL contexts.

The Southeast Asian Ministers of Education Organization (SEAMEO) consists of Brunei Darussalam, Cambodia, Indonesia, Laos, Malaysia, Myanmar, The Philippines, Singapore, Thailand, Timor, and Vietnam. Some of these are impoverished nations where local aspects of English language teaching need development and support without excessive reliance on foreign "experts" and unsuitable methodologies. The aim of SEAMEO is to promote cooperation in education, science, and culture in the region covered by these countries. A recent language teaching conference organized under the aegis of the Organization listed seven invited speakers of whom only two were from the region and only two appeared to be NNS of English. A conference organized by the same organization this year listed 11 invited speakers, five from the USA, one from Australia, one from the UK, one from Spain, one from Germany, one from Spain, and one each from Singapore and Thailand. Only two appeared to be NNS of English. A conference titled "Facing EFL challenges," in neighboring Thailand, included nine keynote speakers. Ironically, five were from the USA, two were from the UK, and one was from New Zealand, clearly not EFL contexts. Only one keynote speaker was based in Thailand, the Country Director of the British Council, and, not surprisingly, a NS of English.

Intrinsic Challenges Faced by NNS English Teachers

Both my wife and I began our careers as English teachers in Sri Lanka. We have a common first language, which is Sinhala, but we frequently converse in English. When I was a graduate student in Texas in the 1980s, a classmate, a NNS speaker and an English teacher, happened to be visiting when my wife called me on the phone. We spoke briefly in English. After I hung up and turned to my classmate, I saw that he was indignant. "You spoke in English!" he cried. I patiently explained to him that my wife and I often speak in English and that we did so because it came quite naturally to us. After all, as English teachers, the English language was part of our identity too, and we spoke and read in English, listened to English songs, and watched English movies. My classmate seemed surprised by my explanation that my wife and I actually used English, the language which provided our livelihood, on a daily basis.

About 15 years after the above incident, I conducted a study in Hong Kong to investigate the academic literacy of graduate students from Mainland China pursuing research degrees in Hong Kong. Since Hong Kong's handover to China in 1997, thousands of students from the mainland have been enrolling at Hong Kong universities. Graduate students, almost all of them on scholarships and assistantships, usually receive support for two years to complete Master of Philosophy degrees and three to four years of support for doctorates. Except in a few disciplines, all degrees are completed in the English medium.

Hong Kong, in contrast to Mainland China, uses English in all aspects of everyday life. English newspapers and magazines are widely read, radio stations broadcast in English throughout the day and night, and two TV channels are in English. Hong Kong is a leading international business center and most business is conducted in English. Except at one university, the medium of instruction of tertiary education is English.

My subjects included seven English majors from both literature and applied linguistics. When asked about the extent of their English use in Hong Kong, these students stated that it was limited to their academic reading and writing. Most never read an English newspaper, never listened to English programs on radio or watched English TV, or read anything in English for pleasure. They only spoke in English with their thesis advisors, and only if the latter happened to be non-Chinese speakers. They had no use for English other than for academic purposes.

To cite a third anecdote, I recently met a graduate of the university where I teach who had taken up an English teaching position in a leading government secondary school. I have known this former student for more than six years, having chosen her to help with my research when she was only a first-year undergraduate because of her high proficiency in English. I later supervised her research at the Masters' level. She is highly proficient in English communicative skills, and well versed in speaking and pragmatic use of the language. The school where she teaches employs more than 15 English teachers, all of them locals except for one NS. My former student told me that she feared she would lose her English proficiency if she continued to teach at this school. None of the English teachers conversed with each other in English. Formal meetings of the English teachers, called the English Panel, were conducted entirely in Cantonese. The only opportunity she had of conversing in English was with the NS teacher, and that wasn't often. Because of a heavy teaching schedule and more time taken up for lesson preparation and grading of student papers, she had no time to read for pleasure in English.

In some ways, the anecdotes and the research cited above, although disappointing, should not have surprised me. During my long-term association with English teachers who are NNS in Hong Kong and elsewhere, I am disturbed by the lack of commitment to English by many of my NNS colleagues and graduate students. These are professionals or professionals in the making who will have a lifelong relationship with the English language and for whom English is their bread and butter. Yet, in their day-to-day lives, the English language plays only a minor role.

Returning to the situation in Hong Kong, where the government pours millions of dollars into the English language curriculum, the local English teachers, all of whom are nonnative speakers, are under siege. A perennial issue in Hong Kong in the past two decades has been the "decline" of English standards among Hong Kong students (Bolton, 2002). As a result of public concern about the low proficiency of language teachers, the government launched a language benchmark test (English Language Proficiency Assessment for Teachers (LPAT)) in 2001. English teachers are tested on reading, writing, listening, speaking, and classroom language assessment. The objective of benchmarking is to make sure that all English teachers possess the minimum proficiency to teach English and to encourage them to strive for higher levels of language proficiency.

In 2001, when the results of the first test were announced, faith in local English teachers was further shaken. Overall, the teachers did not do well, particularly in writing and speaking. Only 33% of the candidates passed in writing, and only half passed in speaking. Local newspapers had a field day, with headlines like "Teachers flunk English test" and "Must do better." In the second benchmarking tests, held in 2002, the pass rates were even lower. Fewer than 30% of the candidates passed in writing and fewer than 40% in listening. More recently, benchmark test have not been any better. In 2005, the pass rate in Writing remained at only 30% and for speaking at 39%, although the rate for listening showed a significant improvement, rising to 64%. After the results of the 2006 benchmark test were announced, about 1,500 English teachers were found to be unsuitable to teach English. They would have to teach other subjects or find employment elsewhere (Clem, 2006).

The Hong Kong government wants to promote English because English is the key to maintaining Hong Kong's position as an international business center, rivaling Singapore and emerging cities in China such as Beijing and Shanghai. The English proficiency of Hong Kong's English teachers, especially those teaching in government primary and secondary schools, has always been worrisome. This low proficiency, common to a large number of indigenous English teachers across Asia, is the intrinsic challenge that NNS teachers face.

What about teachers and teacher trainees in other countries? The proficiency level of English teachers in Sri Lanka has been falling alarmingly. This hardly comes as a surprise because a recent survey showed that very few English teachers read English newspapers or did any type of reading for pleasure. They used English mainly during classroom teaching. An experienced teacher trainer in Sri Lanka once told me that some of her trainees spoke Pidgin English. The situation is similar in other countries. A Panamanian teacher trainer stated that many English teachers in rural Panama only used English in the classroom, to teach the same classes using the same textbooks as they had done for years. We hear the success stories of those who have succeeded, and the need for critical pedagogy and other trendy issues in ESL contexts. But the proficiency level of the majority of English teachers in peripheral EFL countries would shock many of us.

Probably the most powerful intrinsic challenge facing NNS English teachers is the anxiety about their own accents. In Chapter 3 I discussed a study conducted by Jenkins (2005) that highlighted some NNS English teachers' feelings of inferiority about their own accents and their high regard for NS English accents. During lengthy interviews with Jenkins, these teachers had nothing good to say about NNS accents while they described NS accents in complimentary terms. However, a study by Kelch & Santana-Willamson (2002) indicated that ESL students, to whom their teachers' accents would matter the most, were not able to accurately determine NS and NNS English accents.

Perhaps the most impassioned case for lifting the burden of anxiety that NNS English teachers bear has been made by Rajagopalan (2005) who describes how NNS teachers have become marginalized due to systematic campaigns in the guise of academic research that has elevated NS as the true custodians of the language and the only reliable sources for ESL and EFL learners. In the past, under the influence of generative grammar, the superiority of the NS was reinforced even during the professional training of NNS teachers. Resigned to second-class status, these teachers become accustomed to low self-esteem and the associated job-related stress.

Based on his first-hand observations and surveys of more than 400 NNS English teachers in Brazil, Rajagopalan states that because they were not NS of English, the teachers were worried about being under-prepared, undervalued in their profession, handicapped in career advancement, and treated as "second-class citizens" at their workplaces. These worries suggest that the teachers are under constant psychological pressure because they are NNS. Based on his interactions with teachers at a large, privately run English language institute in Brazil, Rajagopalan claims that the inferiority complex felt by NNS is more widespread than at first appearance and emphasizes the need to "re-program" NNS teachers away from the "native speaker fallacy." Rajagopalan ends his appeal with a rousing call: "NNSTs of the world wake up, you have nothing to lose but your nagging inferiority complex" (p. 300).

Chapter 9

Where Does the NNS Movement Go From Here?

The overall impression of NNS English teachers that may have emerged from the previous chapters is that many of them, especially those teaching in EFL or Expanding Circle countries, may be wanting in English language competence. Insecure as NNS of English, they may also suffer from an inferiority complex leading to stress at work. So, as we celebrate the success of the NNS movement in gaining due recognition for these teachers' pedagogical and professional abilities, we need to look more closely at making them more competent and confident users of the English language. In this chapter I will address this matter along with a number of other issues that need attention as the NNS movement continues to grow and become more influential in the field of English language teaching.

Enhancing the English Language Proficiency of NNS Teachers

At the outset, a clearer understanding of the term "proficiency" is needed. Bachman (1990) defines language proficiency as "knowledge, competence, or ability in the use of a language, irrespective of how, where, or under what conditions it has been acquired" (p. 16). This definition, although it includes more terminology such as "knowledge," "competence," and "ability," which in turn need to be defined, is nevertheless open enough to encompass the common-sensical observation that both NS and NNS are capable of attaining proficiency in any language and that language users could have different levels of proficiency in listening, reading, speaking, and writing.

The terms "proficiency" and "fluency" are often used interchangeably when describing language learners. For instance, fluency in speaking a language indicates a speaker's ability as a listener as well as a sound knowledge of slang and idiom. As Pasternak & Bailey (2004) point out, fluency in speaking does not mean that a speaker has mastered grammar and pronunciation. On the other hand, a language user who is not highly proficient in speech may have mastered writing, based mainly on his or her high proficiency in reading. This indicates that language proficiency and fluency could exist at various levels in the four skill areas.

Low levels of proficiency or fluency do not suffice for language teachers because they are not mere users of a language; they are its teachers and role models for students. As an administrator of a Master's program in applied linguistics, I occasionally observe English lessons conducted by NNS teachers in Hong Kong. I am usually satisfied with these teachers' grasp of teaching methodology and classroom management, but the overall impression I have is that the main objective of the lesson—the teaching of English—often receives less emphasis than methodology and classroom management. In fact, in the hands of teachers who are unsure of their own mastery of English, the students may be receiving confusing if not erroneous versions of English.

When do language teachers become "good" teachers? Freeman (1989), a highly experienced teacher educator, describes language teaching as a "decision-making process based on four constituents: knowledge, skills, attitude and awareness" (p. 27). These four elements of language teaching may provide some insights into what makes a good language teacher, but, from our viewpoint, what is significant is that knowledge is listed over skill. Andrews & McNeill (2005), who have extensive teacher-training experience with both NS and NNS teachers, state that for NNS English teachers, their perceived lack of knowledge about language causes much anxiety and that terms such as "fear" and "panic" are "not uncommon" when these teachers express their concerns. As stated earlier, Andrews and McNeill claim that even language teachers who obtain a distinction for the practicum component of their professional training could benefit from courses that enhance their language awareness.

Discussing the relative merits of NS and NNS English teachers, Pasternak and Bailey (2004) refer to the useful distinction between declarative knowledge (knowledge about something) vs. procedural knowledge (the ability to do things, skills). When applied to English language teaching, an example of declarative knowledge is the ability "to explain grammar rules and their exceptions" (p. 158); an example of procedural knowledge is the "ability to use grammar rules appropriately in speaking and writing" (p. 158). Having learned English grammar for many years as primary and secondary students, many NNS teachers may possess sufficient declarative knowledge of grammar. But, lacking in procedural knowledge, these teachers would continue to make errors in speaking and writing. Further, as I had observed with some Hong Kong teachers of English, although most NNS English teachers may have mastered teaching methodology—such as the ability to explain a classroom activity to students and the skill to set up such an activity in small groups—their effectiveness in the classroom may be hampered by shortcomings in the declarative and procedural knowledge of the language.

The distinction between declarative and procedural had been articulated much earlier through the language awareness movement, which has been a major concern of language education since the 1980s.[1] Language awareness has been defined as the relationship between implicit (intuitive) and explicit (conscious) knowledge of a language.[2] According to R. Ellis (2005), for second language users, implicit knowledge is "procedural, is held unconsciously and can only be verbalized if it is made explicit" (p. 214). In essence, implicit knowledge enables "a language user to communicate with confidence and fluency" (Andrews, 2007, p. 14). Explicit knowledge, on the other hand, is declarative knowledge of "the phonological, lexical, grammatical, pragmatic and socio-critical features of an L2" (Ellis, R, 2004, p. 244). Explicit knowledge is held consciously and is learnable, can be verbalized, and is usually "accessed through controlled processing when second language learners experience … difficulty when using the L2" (p. 245).

Teacher language awareness (TLA) is the "knowledge that teachers have of the underlying system of the language that enables them to teach effectively" (Thornbury, 1997, cited in Andrews, 2007). In the case of second-language teachers (both NS and NNS), Andrews explains TLA as a set of knowledge bases that consists of knowledge *of* language (i.e. language proficiency), knowledge *about* language (i.e. declarative knowledge of subject matter), and knowledge of learners. Applying TLA to the NS and NNS debate, Andrews points out that, in terms of knowledge about the language, "NNS teachers are generally assumed to be superior to NSs" (p. 222), although he acknowledges that this may not be the case necessarily. Because NNS teachers may be better at predicting their students' difficulties (as long as they share a common L1 with the students), NNS teachers may also have an advantage in terms of knowledge of the learners, thereby giving NNS an advantage over NS teachers "in two of the three knowledges that make up TLA" (p. 222).

The challenge, therefore, is to enhance the "implicit knowledge/procedural knowledge/knowledge of the language" of NNS English teachers. As pointed out earlier, the vast numbers of English as a second language and as a foreign language speakers, 375 million and 750 million respectively (see www.britishcouncil.org/english/engfaqs.htm) could only be taught by indigenous NNS English teachers. As we have seen through some of the research and anecdotal evidence cited in this volume as well as in the biography of the teacher from Mainland China in Chapter 6, many NNS English teachers appear to be stagnating in terms of their language proficiency because they have ceased to acquire the language.

As professionals, English teachers know the power of language acquisition as opposed to learning. In order to acquire a language, they must read widely, speak the language at every opportunity, participate in conversations, and watch TV and movies. They preach this to their students and their children, continually reminding them of the importance of exposure to English. But, many of them rarely buy and read English newspapers or magazines, or read a novel or a non-fiction book for pleasure, or watch an English movie. Simply stated, they do not practice what they preach.

Next to the fear of speaking in accents, especially when NS are present, writing in English offers the biggest challenge to NNS. Many NNS English teachers are not good writers; I know English teachers, some with Master's or doctoral degrees, who are incapable of drafting an e-mail message without making errors in grammar and word choice. Research has shown fairly conclusively that more reading leads to better writing and that leisure reading or reading for pleasure is a significant enhancer of writing quality (see Ferris & Hedgcock, 2005). But, how many of these teachers actually read for pleasure? As teachers, they have to read school textbooks. As graduate students or scholars, they read reference books or academic articles. But, they seldom read an English newspaper, magazine, or a novel for pleasure. I have visited the households of English teachers in the West as well as in Asia that are like cultural deserts as far as English reading material is concerned. There isn't an English book, a magazine, or a newspaper in sight.

Icy Lee, a teacher educator in Hong Kong, has written about the need for language improvement among her students enrolled in a postgraduate diploma in education program and of the measures she has taken to address these needs (2004). Lee states that the criticism of the declining English standards of NNS English teachers in Hong Kong was of real concern to her students who were preparing to teach in primary and secondary schools and that many of them acknowledged that they did not have a good command of English.

In addition to encouraging her students to join optional language courses designed to enhance English proficiency, Lee gave them questionnaires to determine their learning styles and learning strategies and also raised their consciousness about the use of language strategies. By writing weekly dialog journals, Lee states that the students realized the usefulness of writing practice from the viewpoint of learners and also how one's writing improves with writing practice. Lee also encouraged her students to read extensively by recommending books for leisure reading. To raise her students' language awareness, Lee recommended specific grammar books that the students could read and use as references.

Learning to Collaborate with NS English Teachers

Relations between NS and NNS English teachers could be better. Long relegated to a second-class citizenship in the English teaching profession, many NNS English teachers have looked upon NS English teachers not as colleagues but as threats to their status in the profession, their jobs, and therefore to their economic wellbeing. Despite a mass of evidence to the contrary, the "native speaker fallacy" lives on in the minds of program administrators, parents of students, and the students themselves.

NS and NNS English teachers do not serve together at every institution. Despite various efforts by numerous volunteer organizations, and despite the penetration of the most unlikely locales by backpacking jobseekers, not every school in Africa, Asia, or South America has the resources to attract a NS to teach English. But, in Hong Kong, Japan, South Korea, and Thailand (to name a few Asian contexts), NS English teachers are hired on a formal basis in both primary and secondary schools. This opens the possibility for collaboration between the NS English teachers and local teachers of English, almost all of whom are NNS.

In Hong Kong, NS English teachers have reported problems when teaching low-ability students who are generally not motivated to study English, including disciplinary issues. Their inability to use the students' mother tongue was also seen as a disadvantage. NNS English teachers, on the other hand, saw their NS counterparts as threats to their self-esteem or as being too critical of their pedagogical practices (Carless & Walker, 2006).

Team teaching, defined as "two teachers together in the classroom, actively involved in instruction" (Carless & Walker, 2006, p. 464), appears to be one of the most effective means of collaboration, whether between novice and experienced teachers or NS and NNS teachers. Using a case study method, Carless & Walker observed two NS English teachers who had team taught lower secondary classes with two NNS English teachers for four years in Hong Kong. The NS teachers were experienced teachers from Australia and Ireland, the first a highly experienced language arts teacher and teacher adviser, and the second with three years' teaching English in Japan before coming to Hong Kong. During one class that was observed, the NS teacher took the leading role when oral skills predominated and both the NS and NNS teachers demonstrated dialogs or modeled verbal interactions. The NNS teacher's contribution was to utilize the students' mother tongue to ensure that the lesson flowed smoothly. For instance, the NNS teacher explained the aims of the lesson, solicited Chinese translations for new vocabulary, and worked with weaker students during group work.

During follow-up interviews, NNS teachers acknowledged that team teaching was advantageous to them in a number of ways, such as by enhancing some aspects of their English proficiency and increasing their teaching repertoire. Team teaching was advantageous to students too. While the presence of the NS teacher ensured that students were exposed to more extended and complex speech, the presence of two teachers provided varied input and what Carless & Walker term "higher situational authenticity" arising from the interactions between the two teachers when compared with the "stilted" dialogs in the textbooks. They also observed higher levels of "intellectual engagement" by students and a higher level of teacher support for students in team-taught classes.

George & Davis-Wiley (2000) cite four essential features of teaching partnerships: the mutual satisfaction of gaining something from the partnership; a degree of selflessness from each partner; a willingness to sacrifice or compromise for mutual benefit; and some dissimilarity between the partners so that they could complement each other. As Carless & Walker (2006) have shown, team teaching by NS and NNS is another way in which the English language proficiency and the self-confidence of NNS English teachers could be enhanced.

Making the Most of Professional Organizations

The field of English language teaching—in terms of textbooks publishers, journals, teacher training programs, and teacher organizations—is dominated by British and American interests. This dominance of the ELT profession by British and American interests affects indigenous (NNS) English teachers in various ways. What most English teachers in the West take for granted—membership of international organizations, attendance of international conferences, subscriptions to academic journals, and access to computers and the Internet—are not within the means of many English teachers from less privileged countries. This not only isolates them from mainstream ELT but also inhibits their professional growth.

For instance, the two dominant teacher organizations in the world are the International Association of Teachers of English as a Foreign Language (IATEFL), based in Britain, and Teachers of English to Speakers of Other languages (TESOL), based in the United States. Although both IATEFL and TESOL boast of members worldwide,[3] the overall membership is dominated by local (British and American) members. For instance, the membership breakdown for TESOL shows this imbalance clearly: at the time of writing, 9,209 (76.8%) members were from the United States, while China, India, and Indonesia—three of the most populous countries in the world and countries which have hundreds of thousands of local NNS English teachers—had only 118 members (just 1%) combined (see www.tesol.org). This is despite TESOL's generous offer of Global Memberships and Global Electronic Memberships costing US$40 and US$25 respectively.

Perhaps a personal anecdote might illustrate the important role of professional organizations. I began my English teaching career in Sri Lanka at a time when there were no professional associations there for English teachers. All we had were trade unions, who, to their credit, constantly locked horns with the Ministry of Education and other administrators to ensure salary rights, equitable promotions, and other matters related to our work. However, professional growth in the form of in-service workshops and overseas scholarships were the responsibility of the Ministry, not the trade unions. In 1985, my second year in the United States, I attended the annual TESOL convention which was held in New York. What amazed me was the power, influence, and organizational ability of English teachers and a professional association which brought them together to claim their rights as well as promote their professional growth. The scholarships, academic journals and books, travel awards, and workshops that were available to TESOL members were impressive and overwhelming.

With a feeling of sadness, I pondered the plight of my colleagues back home and the hundreds and thousands of English teachers from similarly underprivileged societies who had no access to an organization like TESOL, Inc.

To their credit, IATEFL and TESOL, Inc. have reached out to English teacher organizations across the world, lending their support and expertise to encourage professional growth and enhance English language teaching. IATEFL has about 70 associates, defined as another teacher association that has entered into a mutually beneficial relationship with IATEFL. The structure and forum for associates are provided by IATEFL and the associates are responsible for making the most of these electronic, print, and face-to-face lines of communication for their own benefit.

TESOL, Inc. has nearly 100 affiliates with a total membership of 47,000 that are autonomous associations affiliated with TESOL and each other, offering English language teachers professional information and support within their geographic regions. These affiliates thus have the opportunity to improve language teaching though the "exchange of ideas, resources, information, newsletters, and reflective experiences" that take place through online discussions, partnerships, conferences, and workshops (see www.tesol.org). The annual TESOL convention brings affiliate representatives together for discussions, workshops, and meetings. Although half the affiliate organizations are located in North America, about 30 are located in Asia, Central and South America, and in the Middle East and Africa. For a nominal fee, TESOL Inc. supports affiliates by extending complimentary memberships, supporting speakers for affiliate conferences, and providing travel grants to affiliates' representatives to attend TESOL conventions.

Although most English language teachers live and work in Asia, until recently there was no organization similar to IATEFL or TESOL Inc. for the region. This need was fulfilled about six years ago with the formation of Asia TEFL, which appears to be a loosely knit organization with affiliates in Indonesia, Japan, Korea, Malaysia, Singapore, and Thailand. Although lacking the formal strucure of IATEFL and TESOL, Inc., Asia TEFL has organized seven annual conferences to date, in venues ranging from Beijing to Bali, attracting hundreds of participants from Asia and around the world. By 2008, membership from the Asian region numbered over 10,000 with another 450 members from around the world. Asia TEFL also publishes a refereed online journal, *The Journal of Asia TEFL*, now in Volume 6.

Yet many NNS English teachers in EFL contexts seem to be oblivious of the benefits provided by professional organizations. Weary from hours of teaching students who appear to be unmotivated to learn English, and unappreciated and unrewarded professionally by local administrators and parents, these teachers prefer to reclaim their lives away from English teaching when they leave for home from school. Instructions on day-to-day classroom teaching, curricula, and textbooks are formulated and handed down by administrators who are seen by many of these teachers as being unaware of the ground realities of English language teaching. Avenues must be found to reach these teachers and convince them that membership and active roles in professional associations will establish a sense of comradeship with fellow English teachers who are mainly NNS, enhance their links to the wider world of English language teaching, and help them overcome any sense of isolation and disillusionment with the profession. In a nutshell, this will lead to their empowerment.

Diversifying the Scope of Research on NNS English Teachers

In Chapters 3, 4, and 7, I summarized and reviewed the research on NNS English teachers. Chapter 3 focused on studies that investigated the self-perceptions of these teachers and Chapter 4 on the way they have been perceived by students. Chapter 7 discussed research beyond self- and student perceptions and served as a follow-up to Chapters 5 and 6 which were biographies of two English teachers from the Outer and Expanding Circles.

A common feature of most studies is that they have been conducted by NNS themselves. This, no doubt, is an indication of the empowerment of these researchers, who are no longer hesitant to acknowledge themselves as NNS and venture into previously uncharted territory. On the other hand, as I have noted earlier (Braine, 2005a), research by NNS on issues that are critical to themselves may cast a shadow of doubt on the validity and reliability of the data and outcomes. Research conducted collaboratively by NS and NNS colleagues is the answer to this quandary. So, what is needed is not only a more robust line of inquiry but also diversification of research areas.

Another shortcoming of the research is that most are one-shot studies that provide hardly any indication of the apprenticeship of NNS to English language teaching, the day-to-day challenges they face as both users and teachers of English, their relationship with the English language beyond the classroom, their professional growth, and their place in society. In essence, what is needed are more longitudinal descriptions (call them ethnographies or case studies for lack of a better term), similar to those of the NNS English teachers in Chapters 5 and 6 of this volume. Inner Circle ESL contexts are fertile grounds for research because of the availability of research grants, technical resources, trained research assistants, and ready outlets for publications. Most Outer and Expanding Circle contexts, on the other hand, lack the resources that Inner Circle researchers take for granted. But, the vast majority of NNS English teachers live and work in these contexts with limited resources and the challenge is to ensure that NNS teachers and their teaching is investigated in longitudinal studies. Such studies do not require expensive equipment; small research grants, with some assurance of the results seeing the light of day in the form of publications, would go a long way to encourage such research.

In addition to longitudinal case studies of NNS English teachers in EFL contexts, what other areas should be the focus of new lines of research? For a start, we could avoid areas of research that are already saturated, such as key features, both positive and negative, that distinguish NS from NNS, self-perceptions of NNS teachers, and students' perceptions of these teachers. In fact, in some EFL contexts where NS English teachers are a rarity, such research is not feasible or relevant. But, research that investigates the ideal qualities and competencies of the NNS English teachers, strategies for overcoming the linguistic barriers faced by NNS English teachers in specific linguistic and cultural contexts, strategies for becoming more competent English teachers beyond basic linguistic competence, the effectiveness of western teaching methodologies in EFL contexts in the hands of NNS English teachers, and the place of local cultural, economic, and linguistic contexts in the training of NNS English teachers are some research areas that come to mind.

Chapter 10

Professional Development

Professional development is a broad topic mainly because the starting point of development has to be defined first. Are we aiming at novice teachers who are at the beginning of their careers or at young scholars who are starting out on their graduate work? On the other hand, is development more relevant to novice scholars who have completed their graduate studies and are on the threshold of academic publications? Whole books have been written on professional development (Bailey, Curtis, & Nunan, 2001, for instance) so a certain degree of narrowing is required if only a chapter is to be written. Hence, this chapter will be aimed mainly at readers who are beginning their research degrees and at novice scholars who are setting out on their academic publications.

Embarking on Research

Research and publication is an inescapable part of the academic world. Initially a requirement for promotion and tenure in the United States and Britain, scholarly publications are now recognized as a notable sign of professional growth and a requirement for academic jobs and promotion in most other countries too. But research is not conducted in a vacuum solely for the purpose of generating publications. I sometimes wonder why a research student would select a particular topic for his/her research. Is it an interesting publication that provoked critical reflection and inspiration? Or is it curiosity about an interesting phenomenon in language acquisition or learning? Or would it be an inner questioning of a theory and the need to find empirical research to support one's position?

Finding a Research Topic

In the mid-1980s, I began teaching writing for the first time in the Freshman Writing program at the University of Texas at Austin. In Sri Lankan primary and secondary schools, during undergraduate years, and during a Masters' degree taken in the United States, I had not been taught writing explicitly.

Writing, it was assumed, is a skill students would "pick up" through practice; one would learn to write by writing. However, as I taught Freshman Writing, I realized that writing could actually be taught, and began to apply my teaching to my own writing. The importance of thesis statements, topic sentences, cohesion and coherence, and the need to support one's position on a topic with plausible evidence—key ingredients of writing that I may have known and practiced instinctively—gradually became consciously applied in my writing process. I knew that my doctoral research would be on some aspect of writing. But which aspect?

Then came Daniel Horowitz's groundbreaking article in *TESOL Quarterly*, "What professors actually require: Academic tasks for the ESL classroom" (1986). The elegance of his research design, the clear organization of ideas, and the smooth writing style had instinctive appeal. I took the opportunity to write to Horowitz and he graciously responded with thoughtful advice on where to go and what to avoid. I decided to investigate the writing assignments given by professors in engineering and the natural sciences and replicated Horowitz's methods in my own research design. In the parlance of English for specific purposes (ESP), I conducted a needs analysis. With Horowitz's support, I also published an article based on the pilot study of my research in *English for Specific Purposes* (Braine, 1989).

Relationships with Thesis Supervisors

A knowledge of one's chosen field of study, research skills, and good reading and writing skills form only the foundation for successful graduate studies. To build upon this foundation, graduate students must adapt quickly to both the academic and social culture of their host environments, and the personalities and demands of their teachers, thesis supervisors, and classmates. Topmost among these is their relationship with the thesis advisor which could even be more important than finding a suitable research topic discussed in the previous section.

Only a few studies have referred to this relationship between NNS graduate students and their thesis supervisors or advisors. Belcher (1994) revealed that thesis advisors and advisees may have distinct notions of culture that could be irreconcilable, that some students may be prone to display their self-assumed brilliance as scholars, as opposed to fulfilling the instructions of their advisors, and that lengthy written criticisms of student writing by advisors may not help the writers. Most importantly, Belcher found that, as far as relationships between advisors and advisees are concerned, dialogic was preferable to hierarchical relationships. A student becomes more receptive to an advisor when the latter assumes a "co-worker and a co-learner" (p. 32) role. Dong (1996), who studied three Chinese students, noted the importance of a hands-on approach by the advisor on the students' research and writing, such as in providing careful guidance in the selection of a research topic and help with writing the theses.

This was more effective than "probing in the dark and learning from mistakes," which students resorted to without adequate guidance from supervisors (see also Li, 1999). The research reveals that a sound relationship between the advisor and advisee is essential to the latter's success, and that, in the case of NNS graduate students, hand-on help by the supervisor from the conception of a research project to the writing of the thesis is the most effective. In fact, what is needed is a collaborative relationship between the advisor and advisee.

However, the large percentage of "all but dissertation" (ABD) students and drop-outs from doctoral studies, especially in the US, could at least partially be attributed to relationships that failed. On occasion, the power of a single advisor to decide one's fate could become an emotionally harrowing experience for a student. I am aware of one advisor who delayed signing a dissertation till his NNS advisee completed his assigned work on a dictionary that the advisor was compiling. In frustration, the student threatened to sue the university and this finally paved the way for his graduation. In my case, of the two advisors who co-chaired my dissertation committee, one took a hands-off approach from the start. It was the generous help of the other advisor that carried me through.

Graduate students often have the option of choosing their thesis advisors. In Hong Kong, I have observed how students hero-worship well known professors and choose them as thesis advisors. These relationships are often detrimental to the students in a number of ways. The professors, because they advise many graduate students, are inundated with work and have little time for hands-on support. As a result, students may have to change their research plans unexpectedly, revise their drafts more frequently because of poor feedback, and even lose enthusiasm for their research. Such students rarely finish their degrees on schedule, don't publish their research, and, after graduation, fade into oblivion.

Students would be prudent to choose professors who have fewer thesis supervisions, who have a track record of providing timely feedback to their supervisees, and co-authoring publications with the supervisees. The question is, do such ideal professors actually exist? In fact, they do, but they may maybe difficult to find at every institution. Instead of choosing supervisors based solely on their scholarship and reputation, graduate students would be better served to network with fellow students and alumni.

In Chapter 8 I referred to a study that I conducted in Hong Kong to investigate the academic literacy of graduate students from mainland China pursuing research degrees at Hong Kong universities. As part of the research, I also queried my subjects about their relationship with thesis advisors. Their responses confirmed the research cited above by Belcher (1994) and Dong (1996). These students depended heavily on their thesis supervisors for support and some even expected the supervisors to edit their writing closely, line by line.

They acknowledged that a sound working relationship was the most important criterion for the success of their doctoral work.[1]

The time of thesis writing is probably the busiest and therefore the most challenging for research students. They will conduct research, write their thesis, and perform assigned tasks such as teaching assistantships and research assistantships. Accordingly, they need to balance their workload and time and should not take on too many responsibilities such as volunteer positions in various organizations. Most importantly, they must learn to say "no" when people make unreasonable demands on their time.

In their research, some students attempt to "change the world" by designing wide-ranging, all-encompassing studies. This is unwise. Instead, graduate students should consider their research a beginning, and plan a study that is feasible within their time limit. In the case of qualitative studies, I have seen how students get bogged down by attempting to transcribe every word of every interview they conducted. Instead, first listening to the tapes and transcribing only the sections that are useful—that is, selective transcribing—should be practiced.

Too immersed in their research and data analysis, some graduate students postpone their writing to the every end. This is not wise. For most graduate students, the thesis is the longest piece of writing they have accomplished and it could become a daunting task. I urge my supervisees to begin writing as early as possible, usually with the Literature Review chapter, which for many is the easiest chapter to compose. The Introduction, which is the first chapter of the thesis, should be the last chapter to be written because it predicts what is to come, and researchers may have changed their methodologies in the course of their research.

Academic Publishing

While the writing process itself is a challenge, novice authors need to be aware that the preparation of a manuscript is only the beginning of a journey to publication. Hence, the aim of this section is to present, from my position as both an author and editor of academic books and journal articles, a manuscript reviewer for numerous journals, and a former editor of two academic journals, strategies that authors could use to have their articles published. To illustrate these macro- and micro-level strategies and the publication process, I will mainly use examples from my own writing and editing.

Choose the Right Journal

Perhaps the most important decision that an academic writer faces is in choosing the most appropriate journal for publication. Fortunately, there is a wide choice. The TESOL Inc. website[2] alone lists more than 50 journals in ELT and applied linguistics. Nevertheless, authors need to keep a few factors in mind as they select an appropriate journal. Should it be a highly prestigious journal in one's discipline; a theoretical, empirical, or pedagogical journal; or a local, regional, or international publication? These decisions depend on the topic and scope of the article and the author's objectives and expectations. For instance, an article dealing with a third-year writing class in Japan would not be suitable for submission to *Written Communication*, a journal more likely to publish on a topic which has wider appeal, such as contrastive rhetoric. Again, if a writer has a short publication deadline for meeting the requirements for an annual review or promotion, a journal which has a shorter review and publication period would be more suitable than a journal which takes longer. Of course, a writer may have to compromise on the status of the journal when choosing to publish quickly.

Academic authors need to be aware that the process, from conceptualization to publication, could often take years. Careful planning is therefore important, especially for an author who needs to maintain a continuous research/publica tions record. A quick survey of the journals in ELT and applied linguistics shows that the review and publication periods range widely from journal to journal. While most scholarly journals such as *The Modern Language Journal* and *TESOL Quarterly* take at least three months to have an article reviewed, publications such as the *English Teaching Forum* and *TESL Reporter* take only a month. However, authors must be prepared to face unexpected delays due to items lost in the mail and reviewers' procrastinations.

In addition to the review period, authors must contend with the time required for publication after an article has been accepted. *The Modern Language Journal* and *TESOL Quarterly*, both international refereed journals, take an average of nine months from acceptance to publication. On the other hand, the *English Teaching Forum* and *TESL Reporter* take only six months. Hence, from initial submission to publication, an article could take a minimum of two years in an international refereed journal provided that the article is accepted for publication without revision. However, in my experience, hardly any article falls into this category; hence, authors may often have a longer wait, up to two years or more, to see an article in print. For those who need to keep publishing regularly, the importance of continuous research and writing cannot be emphasized enough.

Another factor in choosing a journal is the type of article one intends to publish. Is the article theoretical, empirical, or pedagogical? Would the article appeal to generalists or to specialists in the skill areas? If pedagogical, would it appeal to a local audience, such as in Hong Kong, an anglophone audience, or an American audience? For a theoretical or empirical article that would appeal to mainly American writing specialists, the *Journal of Second Language Writing* is probably the most appropriate. On the other hand, for a pedagogical article, one could use the *English Teaching Forum* or the *ELT Journal* for an international audience, or *The Language Teacher* for a Japanese audience.

Generate Multiple Articles from the Same Project

I have already mentioned the importance of continuous research and writing—of having publications in the "pipeline." However, many research projects are expensive and time-consuming and take up most of the spare time of young teachers. Few have the funding or the time to carry out a number of projects concurrently. Hence, one way of ensuring continuous publications is to create multiple articles out of a single research project.

Let me begin with a word of caution. In most instances, journals, not the authors, hold the copyright on articles. Hence, the submission of the same manuscript to more than one journal could lead to copyright violations and severe repercussions for the author. Further, the inclusion of large chunks of text from one manuscript in another will also cause similar problems. If more than one manuscript is to be generated from the same (usually large-scale) project, the author should make note of the other manuscripts in the cover letter which accompanies the manuscript. Further, the other manuscripts should be noted and referenced in the manuscript.

To illustrate the generation of multiple publications, let me cite my doctoral dissertation research, which involved needs analysis in engineering and the natural sciences. For this purpose, I collected assignments given in undergraduate courses at a university in the US. Since not all courses required writing, I focused on engineering and natural science courses listed under the university's Writing Across the Curriculum (WAC) program, which required a minimum number of writing assignments in all its courses. While conducting the study, I realized that the previous approaches to needs analysis contained a number of flaws and that I needed to devise a new approach for my analysis. This approach, described in the literature review chapter of my dissertation, became a theoretical article arguing for a new approach to ESP needs analysis.

My data collection and analysis occurred concurrently and I began to see interesting patterns in the data. Hence, using the initial data analysis, I wrote another article which could be termed a pilot study of my dissertation. The dissertation itself, condensed into an article was eventually published as a chapter in an anthology.

A few years after graduation, I supervised a graduate student who was studying WAC courses at the institution where I taught. Although ESP and WAC studies do not always overlap, I saw parallels between her study and my previous research since both focused on WAC courses. This enabled me to co-author an article with her, comparing the structure and effectiveness of WAC programs at the two universities. Later, when I was invited to write a chapter from an anthology on English for academic purposes (EAP), I compared my needs analyses in Sri Lanka, the US, and Hong Kong, which was published in 2001. As Table 10.1 shows, by emphasizing separate aspects of my research and by focusing on different audiences, I was able to generate five publications from my dissertation research.

Table 10.1 Generating multiple publications from a doctoral dissertation

Year	Title	Type of publication
1988	"Academic-writing task surveys: The need for a fresh approach"	Journal article
1989	"Writing in science and technology: An analysis of assignments from ten undergraduate courses"	Journal article
1993	"Writing across the curriculum: A study of faculty practices at two universities" (co-authored)	Journal article
1995	"Writing in engineering and the natural sciences"	Book chapter
2001	"Twenty years of needs analyses: Reflections on a personal journey"	Book chapter

So far, I have discussed two macro-level aspects of publication, the choice of the right journal and the generation of multiple articles from the same project. However, certain micro-level aspects of article preparation, such as paying careful attention to guidelines for authors, the proper use of visuals and statistics, and a reader-friendly presentation are also important if an author is to succeed.

Pay Careful Attention to Manuscript Preparation

No two journals appear to provide the same guidelines to authors. Although the basic differences between British and American publications are the most obvious, even American journals that follow the APA style have fine distinctions that require careful adherence. For instance, *Computers and Composition*, which follows the APA style, requires the first names of authors in the References section. *Applied Linguistics*, which is published in Britain as well as the United States, requires subtle changes from the APA style. Guidelines also provide specific advice on the number of copies of the manuscript to be submitted, how visuals (tables and figures) are to be presented, the maximum number of words of an article, and if the cost of mailing for reviews is to be borne by the author.

Tables and figures, when used appropriately, enhance the attractiveness and readability of articles. However, as an editor, I have noted some authors' fondness for the overuse of tables and figures and others' lack of knowledge of the appropriate use of visuals. For example, one 20-page article which I edited had 17 graphs. The author was persuaded to combine as many graphs as possible before the article was accepted for publication. Another author compressed so much information into a table that it was beyond comprehension, even after numerous readings. A third author, instead of using bar graphs, used pie charts when comparing the performance of students at an exit test.

Other shortcomings occur in the use of statistics. For instance, I recently critiqued a manuscript which used a questionnaire to survey students on their preferences for teachers. Surveys are more suitable for descriptive research and should employ statistics minimally. Instead, the author used sophisticated statistical devices, crowding the manuscript with nine tables packed with statistics. Another shortcoming is the inclusion of the mean or averages without stating their significance (p value). Perhaps the most useful advice on the use of statistics is provided by *TESOL Quarterly*, which publishes detailed guidelines in every issue on how to report studies and conduct analyses.

While careful adherence to guidelines and the proper use of visuals and statistics are important, a reader-friendly presentation will appeal to reviewers. An appealing title, an accurate abstract, and judicious subtitles add to the readability of an article. Even the font style and size play a role in enhancing readability. Some authors use smaller fonts, such as Times, or larger fonts at size 10, which does not make reading any easier. Instead, I recommend a larger font such as Palatino at size 12.

Consider Revision a Learning Process

Being unaware that articles are rarely accepted for publication without revision, new authors are sometimes discouraged when their manuscripts are returned for revision. About a third of the manuscripts that I returned (during my tenure as a journal editor) to authors for revision were not resubmitted. For editors and reviewers, such manuscripts are a waste of time and effort, especially if they have provided extensive and careful comments and suggestions. Revision is actually a learning process, the first exposure of a manuscript to the intended readers. Hence, reviews are best seen as constructive. In fact, some reviewers provide generous comments and suggestions which run into two or three pages, which are extremely useful during revision.

How do editors choose reviewers? Practices vary from journal to journal. In some journals, all the manuscripts are reviewed by the editorial board, which could consist of up to 20 members. In others, the editors may call upon reviewers at large, depending on their knowledge of the reviewers' expertise. For instance, a manuscript dealing with research in contrastive rhetoric will most likely be sent to contrastive rhetoricians. An editor is likely to send a manuscript to an author who has been cited in the references of the manuscript.

Suggestions for revision are made by the reviewers as well as journal editors. In addition to making changes in the manuscript, the editors will require authors to write a separate response, indicating how the suggestions of the reviewers have been handled. A typical letter from an editor may be worded as follows:

> We are pleased to inform you that we would like to publish your paper in an upcoming issue of … if you are willing to address the reviewers' and our concerns. Specifically, we would like you to consider all of the comments provided and include with your revised manuscript a letter

indicating which comments you have dealt with by making changes in your text and which you have chosen not to address and why.

Two reviewers may sometimes offer contradictory suggestions on a revision which places the author in a quandary. In such a situation, the author should not try to please both reviewers and respond only to suggestions that are feasible. Some reviewers even suggest that the author expand the number of subjects in a study, which can only be accomplished if the author is willing to conduct the study all over again. In such instances, the author should clearly justify his/her selective responses to the reviewers' suggestions.

Be Patient During the Review Process

As mentioned earlier, an article may take years from conceptualization to publication. To best illustrate this process, let me present the chronology of one of my articles.

In 1991 I was responsible for starting a first-year writing program for ESL students at a US university. All students in the program were required to take an exit test at the end-of-the-first-year writing course and I soon realized that ESL students in specially designated ESL classes were performing better at the exit test than ESL students who enrolled in mainstream classes along with NS students. Hence, during the 1992–93 academic year, I began to study the students' performance at the exit tests. As part of the study, I also interviewed some students and their teachers. By March 1994, I submitted a manuscript titled "A comparison of the performance of ESL students in ESL and mainstream classes of Freshman English" to a journal. The reviews, received by me in September 1994, recommended that I revise and resubmit the manuscript for further consideration, which I did in March 1995. The revised manuscript also had a new title: "ESL students in Freshman English: ESL versus mainstream classes." However, in May 1995, the manuscript was rejected. The process, from research to the first rejection of the manuscript, had already taken nearly three years. Later, in July 1995, I submitted the manuscript to another journal and was asked to revise and resubmit the manuscript in October 1995. I immediately submitted the revision, and the manuscript was published in April 1996, under the title "ESL students in first year writing courses: ESL versus mainstream classes" (see Table 10.2). Thus, the entire process took nearly four years during which the manuscript was revised repeatedly and had its title changed thrice. What my experience illustrates is that (1) revisions made according to reviewers' guidelines do not guarantee acceptance, and (2) authors need to be patient during the review and publications process. (See Braine, 2003, for another description of a manuscript's journey to publication.)

In conclusion, although the publication process may seem daunting, the proliferation of new journals in applied linguistics and ELT should be an

Table 10.2 The journey of a manuscript

Date submitted or resubmitted	Title of manuscript/article	Decision
March 1994 (First journal)	"A comparison of the performance of ESL students in ESL and mainstream classes of Freshman English"	Revised and resubmitted (September, 1994)
March 1995	"ESL students in Freshman English: ESL versus mainstream classes"	Rejected (May, 1995)
July 1995 (Second journal)	"ESL students in Freshman English: ESL versus mainstream classes"	Revised and resubmitted (October, 1995)
October 1995	"ESL students in first-year writing courses: ESL versus mainstream classes"	Accepted. Published April 1996

encouragement to new authors. If they choose the right journal, pay careful attention to manuscript preparation, consider revision a learning process, and are patient, they will be rewarded.

Here are a few quick tips to keep in mind as you journey through the publishing process:

- Choose the right publication.
- Start with regional publications (*RELC Journal* [SE Asia], *Prospect* [Australia], *JALT Journal* [Japan], *HKJAL* [Hong Kong])
- One study can lead to more than one publication.
- Use clear visuals.
- Follow closely directions given in "Guide/Notes to Contributors."
- Be patient; reviews take time.
- When revising, don't try to please every reviewer.
- Revise and resubmit.

Notes

Chapter 1

1. This is not to imply that Canagarajah's & Liu's status as NNS was the sole criterion for their positions. They have displayed outstanding scholarship and leadership qualities.

Chapter 2

1. During this period, JALT had about 4,000 members and was the largest affiliate of TESOL, Inc.

Chapter 4

1. "Some students think that only native speakers can be good language teachers. Others think that nonnatives can also be efficient teachers. What is your opinion about this issue? Please feel free to provide details and examples."

Chapter 5

1. Johor Bahru is now a major city across the causeway linking Malaysia and Singapore.
2. Malaysia formally came into being on September 16, 1963, consisting of Malaya, Sabah, Sarawak, and Singapore.

Chapter 6

1. For a description of the history of ELT in China, see He (2005).
2. Sihua's family acquired a TV when she was 18. She then began avidly watching Chinese programs such as "Thirst," "Travel to the West," and "Huoyuanjia."
3. In ancient China, students were taught in "Sishu" (private) schools. There was a teacher, a few tables and benches, and a ruler, for punishment. Children were taught the classics, such as the Analects. Memorizing and reciting the texts were the first steps to becoming an official or a scholar. Underachievers were spanked with the ruler. Handed down from generation to generation, this teaching method ("memorization or punishment") is followed to this day. (Jiang Changsheng, personal communication).
4. This habit of memorization sometimes reaches bizarre levels. Students have been known to memorize the *Oxford Advanced Learners' Dictionary* in reverse order. (Jiang Changsheng, personal communication).

5. At the time of Sihua's schooling, the Chinese curriculum was textbook-, teacher-, and test-centered. Teaching was referred to as "spoon feeding" or more derogatively as "Beijing duck stuffing" (Ouyang, 2004).
6. One of the current texts in use at secondary schools is *Go for It*, which has reportedly sold more than 200 million copies.
7. In these programs, subject knowledge was emphasized with teaching methodology receiving much less attention (Ouyang, 2004).
8. No. 1 is normally an indication of a key middle school in the area.
9. Recalling her own experience as a lecturer at Linyi Teachers College, the interviewer describes being asked by the students to assign an "open book" test and to "go home and rest" instead of supervising the test.
10. The English curriculum in secondary schools consists of required and optional courses based on a system of credits and modules. The required modules will aim to cultivate students' four language skills and develop thinking and expression. Students are to choose optional courses according to their interests, specialty and career plans.

Chapter 9

1. See Andrews (1997) for a history of the language awareness movement.
2. In Krashen's (1981) terms, implicit knowledge is acquired and explicit knowledge learned.
3. In October 2009, IATEFL had over 3,500 members in more than 100 countries, and TESOL had over 11,000 members in 149 countries.

Chapter 10

1. Paul Matsuda also provides useful advice to graduate students at http://www.public.asu.edu/~pmatsuda/blog.html
2. http://www.tesol.org → Career → Career Development → Publishing in the Field

References

Amin, N. (1997). Race and identity of the nonnative ESL teacher. *TESOL Quarterly*, *31*, 580–583.

Amin, N. (1999). Minority women teachers of ESL: Negotiating white English. In G. Braine (Ed.), *Non-native educators in English language teaching* (pp. 94–104). Mahwah, NJ: Lawrence Erlbaum.

Andrews, S. (1994). The grammatical awareness and knowledge of Hong Kong teachers of English. (ERIC Document Reproduction Service ED386 066.)

Andrews, S. (1997). Metalinguistic awareness and teacher explanation. *Language Awareness*, *6*, 147–161.

Andrews, S. (2007). *Teacher language awareness*. London: Cambridge University Press.

Andrews, S. & McNeill, A. (2005). Knowledge about language and the "good language teacher." In N. Bartels (Ed.), *Researching applied linguistics in language teacher education* (pp. 159–178). New York: Springer.

Bachman, L. F. (1990). *Fundamental considerations in language testing*. Oxford: Oxford University Press.

Bailey, K. M., Curtis, A., & Nunan, D. (2001). *Pursuing professional development: The self as source*. Boston, MA: Heinle and Heinle.

Bamgbose, A. (1998). Torn between the norms: Innovations in World Englishes. *World Englishes*, *17*, 1–14.

Belcher, D. (1994). The apprenticeship approach to advanced academic literacy: Graduate students and their mentors. *English for Specific Purposes*, *13*, 24–34.

Benke, E. & Medgyes, P. (2005). Differences in teaching behavior between native and nonnative speaker teachers: As seen by the learners. In E. Llurda (Ed.), *Nonnative language teachers: Perceptions, challenges and contributions to the profession* (pp. 195–215). New York: Springer.

Benoit, B. (2003). Teaching essay writing in Japan. *TOEFL Mail Magazine*, *18*. Retrieved March 4, 2007 from http://www.cieej.or.jp/toefl/mailmagazine/backnumber18.pdf

Bolton, K. (2002). Hong Kong English: Autonomy and creativity. In K. Bolton (Ed.), *Hong Kong English: Autonomy and creativity* (pp. 1–25). Hong Kong: Hong Kong University Press.

Bolton, K. (2004). World Englishes. In A. Davies & C. Elder (Eds.), *The handbook of applied linguistics* (pp. 367–396). Oxford: Blackwell.

Boyle, J. (1997). Native-speaker English teachers in Hong Kong. *Language and Education*, *11*, 163–181.

Braine, G. (1989). Writing in science and technology: An analysis of assignments from ten undergraduate courses. *English for Specific Purposes, 8*, 3–15.

Braine, G. (1998). NNS and invisible barriers in ELT. *TESOL Matters, 8*(1), 14.

Braine, G. (Ed.) (1999). *Nonnative educators in English language teaching.* Mahwah, NJ: Lawrence Erlbaum.

Braine, G. (2003). Negotiating the gatekeepers: The journey of an academic article. In C. Pearson and S. Vandrick (Eds.), *Writing for scholarly publication* (pp. 73–90). Mahwah, NJ: Lawrence Erlbaum.

Braine, G. (2005a). A critical review of the research on non-native speaker English teachers. In C. Gnutzman and F. Intemann (Eds.), *The globalization of English and the English language classroom* (pp. 275–284). Tübingen, Germany: Gunther Narr.

Braine, G. (Ed.) (2005b). *Teaching English to the world: History, curriculum, and practice.* Mahwah, NJ: Lawrence Erlbaum.

Butler, Y. G. (2007a). Factors associated with the notion that native speakers are the ideal language teachers: An examination of elementary school teachers in Japan. *JALT, 29*(1), 7–40.

Butler, Y. G. (2007b). How are nonnative English speaking teachers perceived by young learners? *TESOL Quarterly, 41*, 731–755.

Canagarajah, A. S. (1999). Interrogating the "native speaker fallacy": Non-linguistic roots, non-pedagogical results. In G. Braine (Ed.), *Non-native educators in English language teaching* (pp. 145–158). Mahwah, NJ: Lawrence Erlbaum.

Carless, D. & Walker, E. (2006). Effective team teaching between local and native-speaking English teachers. *Language and Education, 20*, 463–477.

Cheung, Y. L. (2002). The attitude of university students in Hong Kong towards native and nonnative teachers of English. Unpublished master's thesis, The Chinese University of Hong Kong.

Cheung, Y. L. & Braine, G. (2007). The attitudes of university students towards non-native speaker English teachers in Hong Kong. *RELC Journal, 38*, 257–277.

Chomsky, N. (1965). *Aspects of the theory of syntax.* Cambridge, MA: MIT Press.

Clark, E. & Paran, A. (2007). The employability of non-native speaker teachers of EFL: A UK survey. *System, 35*, 407–430.

Clem, W. (2006). 2,000 language teachers fail to make grade. *South China Morning Post*, Education Post, May 22, C1.

Davies, A. (1991). *The native speaker in applied linguistics.* Edinburgh: Edinburgh University Press.

Davies, A. (2003). *The native speaker: Myth and reality* Clevedon: multilingual matters.

Derbel, F. (2005). Fully qualified but still marginalized. *Essential Teacher, 2*(1), 10–11.

Dogancay-Aktuna, S. (2008). Non-native English speaking teacher educators: A profile from Turkey. In S. Dogancay-Aktuna and J. Hardman (Eds.), *Global English teaching and teacher education: Praxis and possibility* (pp. 61–82). Alexandria, VA: TESOL Publications.

Dong, Y. (1996). Learning how to use citations for knowledge transformation: Non-native doctoral students' dissertation writing in science. *Research in the Teaching of English, 30*, 428–457.

Ellis, E. (2002). Teaching from experience: A new perspective on the non-native teacher in adult ESL. *Australian Review of Applied Linguistics, 25*, 71–107.

Ellis, E. (2004). The invisible multilingual teacher: The contribution of language background to Australian ESL teachers' professional knowledge and beliefs. *The International Journal of Multilingualism, 1*, 90–108.

Ellis, R. (2004). The definition and measurement of explicit knowledge. *Language Learning, 54*, 281–318.

Ellis, R. (2005). Principles of instructed language learning. *System, 33*, 209–224.

Ferris, D. & Hedgcock, J. (2005) *Teaching ESL Composition* (2nd Edn.). Mahwah, NJ: Lawrence Erlbaum.

Forde, K. (1996). A study of learner attitudes towards accents of English. *Hong Kong Polytechnic University Working Papers in ELT and Applied Linguistics, 1*(2), 59–76.

Freeman, D. (1989). Teacher training, development, and decision making: A model of teaching and related strategies for language teacher education. *TESOL Quarterly, 23*(1), 27–45.

George, M. & Davis-Wiley, P. (2000). Team teaching a graduate course. *College Teaching, 48*, 75–80.

Hayes, D. (2005). Exploring the lives of non-native speaking English educators in Sri Lanka. *Teachers and teaching: Theory and practice, 11*, 169–194.

He, A. E. (2005). Learning and teaching English in the People's Republic of China. In G. Braine (Ed.) *Teaching English to the world* (pp. 11–21). Mahwah, NJ: Lawrence Erlbaum.

Heron, L. (2006). Asian English teachers demand action on racial discrimination. *South China Morning Post*, Education Post, E3.

Horowitz, D. (1986). What professors actually require: Academic tasks for the ESL classroom. *TESOL Quarterly, 20*, 445–462.

Howatt, A. (1984). *A history of English language teaching*. Oxford: Oxford University Press.

Hsu, H. (2005). Mainland bias against Chinese from the west. *South China Morning Post*, November 28, A16.

Inbar-Lourie, O. (2001) Native and nonnative English teachers: Investigation of the construct and perceptions. Unpublished Ph.D. dissertation, Tel Aviv University, Israel.

Inbar-Lourie, O. (2005). Mind the gap: Self and perceived native speaker identities of ELF teachers. In E. Llurda (Ed.), *Non-native language teachers: Perceptions, challenges, and contributions to the profession* (pp. 265–281). New York: Springer.

Jenkins, J. (2005). Implementing an international approach to English pronunciation: The role of teacher attitudes and identity. *TESOL Quarterly, 39*, 535–543.

Kachru, B. (1992). World Englishes: Approaches, issues, and resources. *Language Teaching, 25*, 1–14.

Kamhi-Stein, L. (Ed.) (2004). *Learning and teaching from experience: Perspectives on nonnative English-speaking professionals*. Ann Arbor, MI: University of Michigan Press.

Kamhi-Stein, L., Aagard, A., Ching, A., Paik, A., & Sasser, L. (2004). Teaching in K-12 programs: Perceptions of native and NNEST practitioners. In L. D. Kamhi-Stein (Ed.), *Learning and teaching from experience: Perspectives on Nonnative English-speaking professionals* (pp. 81–99). Ann Arbor, MI: University of Michigan Press.

Kelch, K. & Santana-Williamson, E. (2002). ESL students' attitudes toward native- and nonnative-speaking instructors' accents. *The CATESOL Journal, 14*, 57–72.

Kingston, M. H. (1977). *The woman warrior: Memoirs of a girlhood among ghosts*. New York: Random House.

Kirkpatrick, A. (2006). Blatant racism in the teaching of English. *South China Morning Post*, Education Post, January 21, E4.

Krashen, S. (1981). *Second language acquisition and second language learning*. Oxford: Pergamon.

Lai, M. L. (1999). JET and NET: A comparison of native-speaking English teacher schemes in Japan and Hong Kong. *Language, Culture, and Curriculum, 12*, 215–228.

Lasagabaster, D. & Sierra, J. M. (2002). University students' perceptions of native and non native speaker teachers of English. *Language Awareness, 11*, 132–142.

Lee, I. (2004). Preparing nonnative English speakers for EFL teaching in Hong Kong. In L.D. Kamhi-Stein (Ed.), *Learning and teaching from experience* (pp. 230–249). Ann Arbor, MI: University of Michigan Press.

Li, X. (1999). Writing from the vantage point of an insider/outsider. In G. Braine (Ed.), *Non-native educators in English language teaching* (pp. 43–55). Mahwah, NJ: Lawrence Erlbaum.

Liang, K. Y. (2002). *English as a second language (ESL) students' attitudes toward non-native English-speaking teachers' (NNESTs') accentedness.* Unpublished master's thesis, California State University, Los Angeles.

Liao, X. (2004). The need for communicative language teaching in China. *ELT Journal, 58* (3), 27–73.

Liu, J. (1999). Nonnative English speaking professionals. *TESOL Quarterly, 33*(1), 85–102.

Liu, J. (2001). Writing from Chinese to English: My cultural transformation. In D. Belcher & U. Connor (Eds.), *Reflections on multiliterate lives* (pp. 121–131). Clevedon: Multilingual Matters.

Llurda, E. (Ed.) (2005). *Non-native language teachers: Perceptions, challenges, and contributions to the profession.* New York: Springer.

Llurda, E. & Huguet, A. (2003) Self-awareness in NNS EFL primary and secondary school teachers. *Language Awareness, 12*, 220–235.

Luk, J. (1998). Hong Kong students' awareness of and reactions to accent differences. *Multilingua, 17*, 93–106.

Luk, J. (2001). Exploring the sociocultural implications of the Native English-speaker Teacher scheme in Hong Kong through the eyes of the students. *Asia-Pacific Journal of Language Education, 4*, 19–49.

Lung, J. (1999). A local teacher views the native English teacher scheme in Hong Kong. *TESOL Matters, 9*(3), June/July, 5.

McNeill, A. (2005). Non-native speaker teachers and awareness of lexical difficulty in pedagogical texts. In E. Llurda (Ed.), *Non-native language teachers: Perceptions, challenges and contributions to the profession* (pp. 107–125). New York: Springer.

Mahboob, A. (2003). *Status of nonnative English-speaking teachers in the United States.* Unpublished Ph.D. dissertation, Indiana University, Bloomington, IN.

Mahboob, A. (2004). Native or nonnative: What do students enrolled in an intensive English program think? In L. D. Kamhi–Stein (Ed.), *Learning and teaching from experience. Perspectives on nonnative English-speaking professionals* (pp. 121–147). Ann Arbor, MI: University of Michigan Press.

Mahboob, A., Uhrig, K., Newman, K., & Hartford, B. (2004). Children of a lesser English: Nonnative English speakers as ESL teachers in English language programs in the United States. In L. D. Kamhi-Stein (Ed.), *Learning and Teaching from Experience: Perspectives on Nonnative English-speaking Professionals* (pp. 100–120). Ann Arbor, MI: University of Michigan Press.

Medgyes, P. (1983). The schizophrenic teacher. *ELT Journal, 37*, 2–6.

Medgyes, P. (1992). Native or nonnative: Who's worth more? *ELT Journal, 46*(4), 340–349

Medgyes, P. (1994). *The non-native teacher.* London: Macmillan.

Medgyes, P. (2000). Non-native speaker teacher. In M. Byram (Ed.), *Routledge encyclopedia of language teaching and learning* (pp. 444–446). London: Routledge.

Moussu, L. (2002). English as a second language students' reactions to nonnative English-speaking teachers. Master's thesis, Brigham Young University, Provo (ERIC Document Reproduction Service No. ED 468 879).

Moussu, L. (2006). Native and non-native English-speaking English as a second language teachers: Student attitudes, teacher self-perceptions, and intensive English program administrator beliefs and practices. Ph.D. Dissertation. Purdue University (ERIC Document Reproduction Service No. ED492 599).

Moussu, L. & Braine, G. (2006). The attitudes of ESL students towards nonnative English language teachers. TESL Reporter, 39, 33–47.

Moussu, L. & Llurda, E. (2008). Non-native English-speaking English language teachers: History and Research. Language Teaching, 41, 316–348.

Nemtchinova, E. (2005). Host teachers' evaluations of nonnative-English-speaking teacher trainees: A perspective from the classroom. TESOL Quarterly, 39, 235–261.

Mura, D. (1991). Turning Japanese: Memoirs of a sansei. New York: Atlantic Monthly.

Niu, Q. & Wolff, M. (2004). English as a foreign language: The modern day Trojan horse? Retrieved March 4, 2007 from http://www.usingenglish.com/esl-in-china/

Oda, M. (1999). English only or English plus? The language(s) of EFL organizations. In G. Braine (Ed.), Non-native educators in English language teaching (pp. 105–121). Mahwah, NJ: Lawrence Erlbaum.

Ouyang, H. H. (2004). Remaking of face and community of practices: An ethnography of local and expatriate English teachers' reform stories in today's China. Beijing: Beijing University Press.

Park, Y. (2006). Will nonnative-English speaking teachers ever get a fair chance? Essential Teacher, 3(1), 32–34.

Pasternak, M. & Bailey, K. (2004). Preparing nonnative and native English-speaking teachers: Issues of professionalism and proficiency. In L. D. Kamhi-Stein (Ed.), Learning and teaching from experience (pp. 155–175). Ann Arbor, MI: University of Michigan Press.

Phillipson, R. (1992). Linguistic imperialism. Oxford: Oxford University Press.

Rajagopalan, K. (2005). Non-native speaker teachers of English and their anxieties: Ingredients for an experiment in action research. In E. Llurda (Ed.), Non-native language teacher: Perceptions, challenges, and contributions to the profession (pp. 283–303). New York: Springer.

Reves, T. & Medgyes, P. (1994). The non-native English speaking EFL/ESL teacher's self-image: An international survey. System, 22, 353–367.

Samimy, K. & Brutt-Griffler, J. (1999). To be a native or nonnative speaker: Perceptions of nonnative speaking students in a graduate TESOL program. In G. Braine (Ed.), Non-native educators in English language teaching (pp. 127–144). Mahwah, NJ: Lawrence Erlbaum.

Shao, T. (2005). Teaching English in China: NNESTs need not apply? NNEST Newsletter, 7(2).

Sifakis, N. & Sougari, A. (2005). Pronunciation issues and EIL pedagogy in the periphery: A survey of Greek state school teachers' beliefs. TESOL Quarterly, 39, 467–488.

Soheili-Mehr, A. H. (2008). Native and non-native speakers of English: Recent perspectives on theory, research, and practice. Language Teaching, 41, 445–457.

Suresh, B. (2000). Native English must be a white thing. South China Morning Post, November 15, 17.

Tang, C. (1997). The identity of the nonnative ESL teacher. TESOL Quarterly, 31, 577–580.

Index

eBooks – at www.eBookstore.tandf.co.uk

A library at your fingertips!

eBooks are electronic versions of printed books. You can store them on your PC/laptop or browse them online.

They have advantages for anyone needing rapid access to a wide variety of published, copyright information.

eBooks can help your research by enabling you to bookmark chapters, annotate text and use instant searches to find specific words or phrases. Several eBook files would fit on even a small laptop or PDA.

NEW: Save money by eSubscribing: cheap, online access to any eBook for as long as you need it.

Annual subscription packages

We now offer special low-cost bulk subscriptions to packages of eBooks in certain subject areas. These are available to libraries or to individuals.

For more information please contact webmaster.ebooks@tandf.co.uk

We're continually developing the eBook concept, so keep up to date by visiting the website.

www.eBookstore.tandf.co.uk